THE
PRACTICAL
CIO

THE
PRACTICAL
CIO

A Common Sense Guide for Successful IT Leadership

JOSÉ CARLOS EIRAS

WILEY

John Wiley & Sons Inc.

Published by John Wiley & Sons, Inc., Hoboken, New Jersey.
Published simultaneously in Canada.

For general information on our other products and services or for technical support, please contact our Customer Care Department within the United States at (800) 762-2974, outside the United States at (317) 572-3993 or fax (317) 572-4002.

Wiley also publishes its books in a variety of electronic formats. Some content that appears in print may not be available in electronic books. For more information about Wiley products, visit our web site at www.wiley.com.

Library of Congress Cataloging-in-Publication Data

Eiras, Jose Carlos, 1947-
  The practical CIO : a common sense guide for successful IT leadership / Jose Carlos Eiras.
      p. cm.
  Includes bibliographical references and index.
  ISBN 978-0-470-53190-7 (cloth)
  1. Chief information officers.   2. Information technology–Management.   I. Title.
  HD30.2.E386 2010
  658.4'038–dc22

                                                                2009041465

Printed in the United States of America

10 9 8 7 6 5 4 3 2 1

To my wife, Alzira, for showing me the light many times over.
To my mother, Edit, for always keeping a candle lit for me.

CONTENTS

FOREWORD

Tony Scott
CIO, Microsoft Corp.

Looking over the past quarter century of information technology development, one of the few constants I can observe is continuing change.

From the moment I performed my first chore as a newly hired techie, it seemed as though all of us in IT were constantly framing the decisions in front of us in the context of what we knew was coming next. We just didn't know how fast. The tantalizing future was right around the bend, and we were speeding toward it just as fast as our budgets and human capabilities would allow us to go.

Even as we toiled away over our mainframes, we read and we wondered about and in some cases started getting experience with microcomputers, networks, parallel processing, and distributed computing. Soon we were reading and wondering about servers, data warehouses, OLAP, and XML.

The Internet and the Web browser changed everything, of course, except the rapid pace of change itself. We hurtled into the future, propelled by a volatile mixture of Moore's Law and our own imaginations. Today we are pondering the impact of virtualization and cloud computing. Tomorrow we will be thinking about—who knows? I really cannot think of another field that has experienced so much change in so brief a span of time. The speed at which IT evolves is, quite simply, breathtaking.

For the modern CIO, however, there is one certainty: IT must deliver solutions that enable the business to achieve its goals. IT must be aligned with the business; the goals of IT and the rest of the enterprise must be compatible and mutually supporting. Today's CIO must develop a comprehensive IT strategy that maintains the alignment between IT and the rest of the enterprise. In addition to supporting the business, IT must also be ready to drive the business.

In some ways, the added burdens on IT make me genuinely nostalgic for the good old days when the primary job of IT was taking care of technology and the CEO's primary job was taking care of strategy. The lines of demarcation are not as distinct as they were 25 years ago. As technology evolves into a critical driver of business development, those lines are becoming even less distinct and considerably more blurred.

The extraordinarily rapid pace of business transformation requires the CIO to do a lot more than just determine a path from A to B. The modern CIO must figure out how to get from A to n. And needless to say, the value of n is always changing.

Given the difficulty of the task, where does the CIO begin? Here is my practical advice:

- *Know where you are today.* This might sound simplistic, but you need a complete and precise inventory of your IT department's assets, capabilities, and capacities. You have to know which of your systems are working and which are not. You have to know which applications are nearing the end of their useful lives, and you must have a plan for retiring them. Many CIOs struggle because they do not possess that fundamental knowledge of their own systems.

- *Plan for tomorrow.* An important part of your job is figuring out which technologies will be important six months from now, a year from now, and five years from now. Do you have the infrastructure and the governance in place to support these new technologies? Where will you find the people to run and manage the new systems you will bring on board? As the CIO, you must plan for the future now—it will arrive sooner than you think.

- *Prepare to move smoothly from the present into the future.* This is the hard part, because it requires patience, skill, planning, and a sense of purpose. You must envision all of the many steps required to adopt new technologies while maintaining the alignment between IT and the rest of the enterprise. Then you must execute all of those steps without missing deadlines, going over budget, or inadvertently creating new problems. This is the true test of the CIO's character and ability.

Companies are only now beginning to realize that IT has an exceptional vantage point. Because IT is quite literally *everywhere* in the enterprise, IT tends to *see* everything. Since

IT is embedded in virtually every business process, frictions and inefficiencies in the enterprise become visible through the perspective lens of IT. This is not a metaphor; this is a description of the new reality of business.

More people today generally understand that IT can do more than just keep the trains running on time; IT can deliver insight and intelligence based on information gathered from every corner of the enterprise. The mere fact that IT has a unique view of the enterprise does not grant the CIO magical powers. Whatever influence the CIO wields must be earned the old-fashioned way, by inspiring trust and confidence.

The modern CIO focuses on building relationships and partnerships. The modern CIO also earns respect by delivering on promises and commitments to multiple business partners across the enterprise. The quality of these relationships and partnerships will not be judged by the sleekness of new technologies; they will be judged mainly by the business results that those new technologies make possible. At Microsoft we have a formal process for evaluating the relationships between IT and its business partners. We call this process "shared commitments." It focuses more on business outcomes than on explicit technology goals, and it is measured using our scorecarding methodology. One of the interesting aspects of this process is that it empowers leaders from IT and the business to "stop the assembly line" when they spot minor problems that could lead to bigger problems down the road. Then we all sit down together and try to solve the problem, even if it means missing an internal deadline or delaying the implementation of a new solution. We did not invent this approach; Japanese automakers have been using it for years.

Naturally, this approach can put IT in the hot seat. From our virtual crow's nest, we can often see potential problems sooner than other parts of enterprise. This can lead to some tense meetings between IT and our business partners. But I have noticed over my career that when the new solution is up and running successfully, people tend to forget the minor scraps that invariably took place along the way. What they tend to remember is that when it really counted, IT delivered on its promises and the business achieved its goals.

Obviously, it will be more difficult to build trusting relationships with your business partners if IT is not delivering basic services or is performing inconsistently. At the risk of contradicting my earlier statement, you still have to keep the trains running on time. Unlike the earlier generation of CIOs, today's CIOs are expected to help the enterprise achieve its business goals. That expectation represents a fundamental shift in thinking and it certainly poses the biggest challenge for the current generation of CIOs.

In my bones, I feel another wave of transformation looming over the horizon. It will bring opportunity and disruption. It might make solving today's problems seem like child's play. This book will help you deal successfully with the challenges ahead of you. José Carlos Eiras shared his wisdom generously with me when I worked with him at General Motors, and I benefited greatly from his knowledge and experience. I know that you will too.

ACKNOWLEDGMENTS

This book is based largely on the knowledge and insight that I acquired from over four decades of experience as a senior IT executive at several large companies. But since the book is also a work of journalism and reportage, I could not have completed it without tapping into the collective wisdom of many expert sources. To them I am deeply indebted. I thank them sincerely for their time, their energy, their intelligence, and their support.

I owe a special debt of gratitude to Mike Barlow, the co-author of *Partnering with the CIO* (John Wiley & Sons, 2007). Mike served as my editorial director for *The Practical CIO* and his guidance was truly invaluable. In addition to being a talented writer and communicator, Mike is an all-around good guy. Thank you, Mike!

Esther Schindler, the well-known writer, editor and blog-ger *extraordinaire*, also provided timely support, constructive criticism, and a unique perspective on the continually ex-panding information technology universe. Thank you, Esther!

Much of the content of this book was based on in-depth interviews with CIOs and senior executives at numerous com-panies and organizations all over the world. I could not have written it without the active participation and cooperation of

Ashlee Aldridge, Matthew Chamberlin, Eric Chow, William Christie, Ronald Franz, Michael Hugos, Darwin John, Claudio Joppert, Beth Kirkpatrick, Harvey Koeppel, Mark Lutchen, Claude Marais, Steve Marenakos, Alejandro Martinez, Rita Gunther McGrath, Caroline Michiels, Joseph Miller, Michael Moran, Eugene Nizker, Jim Onalfo, Mark Polansky, Chris Potts, Manjit Singh, Tony Scott, Marco Stefanini, Bob Turner, Cesar Vinocur, Mitch Wagner, Kevin Wale, Robin Watson, Mansour Zadeh, and Dave Zitur.

A special thanks to Jim Giustini for his contribution to the book. Jim helped me a lot when I was CIO of DHL-US. We are now collaborating again at Resources Global, a consulting company that I admire greatly.

All writers, of course, need many additional pairs of eyes. I was especially fortunate to work with Edith G. Barlow, whose initial copy editing and useful suggestions greatly improved the quality of the manuscript. I also thank Sheck Cho and Stacey Rivera, my editors at John Wiley & Sons, who had faith in the value of the project and were patient when I missed my deadlines.

Most of all, I thank my wife, Alzira, who put up with long nights of writing, endless phone calls, and lost weekends of heavy editing.

INTRODUCTION

Rapidly Changing Markets Require Transformative Leadership

I always thought that I was lucky to be born in Brazil, but the real value of my ancestry became apparent to me only after I became Chief Information Officer (CIO) of General Motors Europe. As you can imagine, a lot of my energy was consumed by the process of managing a large, decentralized team that was both multinational and multicultural.

As a native Brazilian, I was considered a "foreigner" by everyone. That perception offered me a cloak of neutrality that came in handy whenever I had to resolve disputes. It also provided me with a unique perspective on the skills required to manage a busy IT shop in a global economy.

Now seems like a good time to share some of the insights that I acquired at General Motors and other global organizations such as DHL, General Foods, Philip Morris, and Kraft Foods. I hope you will find them useful as you confront the challenges of today.

One of the primary differences between today's CIOs and the previous generation of IT leaders is the idea of transformational change. Thirty years ago, nobody seriously believed that IT would be called upon to lead enormous transformational efforts affecting every aspect of a global enterprise. Today, in addition to making sure that IT runs smoothly, the CIO is expected to provide strategic leadership and high-level guidance. That is a big difference indeed.

Welcome to the "New Normal"

We are living in interesting times. Rapid shifts in market dynamics require new modes of thinking and novel approaches to strategy at all levels of the enterprise.

When I began this book, the world economy was unraveling. Now it appears to be heading back toward some level of stability. But the "new normal" is not likely to resemble the "old normal" that we grew accustomed to during the boom times of the 1990s and most of the first decade of the twenty-first century.

The IT landscape will never be the way it was back in "the good old days" when it seemed as though vendors sold their wares by the pound and nobody really understood—or cared about—the value of information technology.

As the global economy evolves and transforms, IT executives face dilemmas of truly mythic proportions. Despite understandable feelings of helplessness, they must still choose their destiny. Whether they emerge as heroes or scapegoats is up to them.

Many CIOs will find themselves trapped in a labyrinth from which there appears no hope of escape. On the one hand, they must focus on cost reduction. On the other hand, they must produce tangible results for the business.

As they strive for cost reduction, their decisions are driven more by panic than logic. Some of those hasty decisions can make it nearly impossible for IT to deliver the results necessary to sustain the business in times of great stress.

As a survivor of four previous recessions, I can testify that hard times present excruciating business challenges. Challenging times also bestow incredible opportunities for building the infrastructures required for future growth.

So you have a choice. Do you hunker down and wait timidly for fate, or do you seize the moment and act like a hero?

To the sacrificial lambs, I offer my condolences. To the would-be heroes, I offer two pieces of advice:

1. Cut IT expenses deeply, but remember to set aside adequate funds for development and revamping of your systems and infrastructure. Think of those funds as seed money for growing the business.

2. Whatever you do, make sure that you keep enough money in the budget for retaining your top performers. They will get you through the hard times.

Even if you stop reading now, I hope that you consider those two pearls of advice and take them to heart. If you do, you will increase your chances of surviving through the next couple of rough quarters. You will also be nicely positioned for the recovery—when it arrives.

For CIOs with genuinely heroic souls, I also offer the following suggestions:

- *Build a great team.* As the manager of an indispensable organization within a larger business, some of your primary responsibilities are attracting, nurturing, promoting, motivating, and preserving talent. The responsibilities to find and manage talent extend well beyond the traditional boundaries of the company to include vendors, consultants, business partners, and all the various outsourcers that IT depends upon. A deep pool of talent is a great asset and the best hedge against the uncertainties of a bad economy.

- *Proactively establish goals for IT.* Don't wait for someone to tell you what to do or you'll always be trailing the pack. In a challenging economy, it's actually easier to set realistic goals and accomplish them than it is during periods of rapid growth. Since all areas of the business are in a cost-cutting mode, now is the perfect time to simplify your IT landscape by eliminating legacy systems and redundant components. Remember, IT owns the systems, so there's no excuse for not acting swiftly when the opportunity arises to ditch a costly and inefficient legacy system and revamp or replace it with a more cost-effective alternative.

- *Design the IT strategy.* Even in the best of times, you could not raise capital for a business unless it had a strategic plan. Think of IT as a business and think of your company's board of directors as a group of venture capitalists. Write out a strategy for IT, share it with the board and use that strategy as the template for everything you do.

- *Hold all of your vendors accountable.* Make certain they are delivering on their promises to you. Remember, they're part of your team. Manage your relationships with them and make sure the contracts you sign reflect *your* business needs and not just the needs of your vendors.

- *Before negotiating do your homework.* Very few CIOs relish the prospect of negotiating contracts with suppliers. Even fewer of them enjoy renegotiating contracts. But in a difficult economy, sometimes you need to bite the bullet, call a supplier and say, "You know, this deal just isn't working." That's when you need all your ducks in a row, because renegotiating a contract requires more than courage—you need to know precisely what you're trying to achieve and be ready to offer alternatives.

- *Manage contracts, don't just sign them.* Negotiating a good contract can be a burdensome chore. But managing a contract is where the real work starts. Just because you have a signed contract with a service provider does not mean that you can put your feet up on your desk and relax. Business conditions can change, rendering some conditions in the contract meaningless. A shift in business strategy might require you to seek new terms. Nothing is chiseled into stone, no matter what the lawyers tell you. Most of all, a contract does not guarantee performance. It is your job to make sure the provider delivers.

- *Work with the business.* The business values results. If you cannot deliver results, the business has no need for you. Once you understand what the business needs in terms of results, you can align IT operations to help the business deliver those results. Work with the business, not for the business.

- *Manage and market the IT brand.* IT is a product and like any other product, it cannot speak for itself. That is where you, the CIO, come in. You must put a face on IT, you must explain to the world what IT does and how it creates value. In other words, you must sell IT. But before you can sell IT, you must learn how to market IT. To the amusement of your colleagues in the marketing department, you are likely to discover that marketing a complicated product such as IT is harder than it looks.

- *Build and manage relationships up, down, and sideways across the enterprise and beyond its traditional boundaries.* Remember that IT is a team effort, and you need cooperation from an extremely wide range of participants, in and out of the organization, to get the most value from your IT systems. Usability and user acceptance will always be critical issues, so don't forget to include the user base in your considerations.

- *Act like a CEO.* CIOs need to define their role broadly. They are the chief executives of complex businesses that exist within larger complex businesses. When you act like the Chief Executive Officer (CEO) of IT, you generate respect for the IT organization. That respect usually translates into more cooperation from all the various constituencies required to keep IT running smoothly. Acting like a CEO also makes it easier for you to sell your programs to other C-suite executives, making it more likely that your budget requests will be approved and funded.

Last but not least, I urge you to think green. Sustainability is more than a trend—it's a smart strategy. IT can play a crucial role in developing, managing, auditing, and analyzing green projects across the enterprise, so do yourself a favor and don't surrender this opportunity to accumulate more responsibility and acquire expertise in an area that will certainly grow in importance.

Drive the Economic Engine

When I began my career back in the early 1970s, I never dreamed that IT would evolve into the indispensable engine of a global economy. Even as the global economy falters and sputters, it seems to me that IT is more significant than ever. This significance puts a heavy burden on the shoulders of CIOs.

A couple of years ago, business academics wondered if CIOs were truly prepared for their roles as C-level executives.

Today, some of these same academics wonder if CIOs are still relevant or even necessary.

From my perspective, CIOs are relevant and necessary. Think about it: Information technology is everywhere, and this is just the beginning of a new era in which some form of digital intelligence will be built into practically every product you can imagine. When you look at the future and consider the potential of information technology, you will see a path stretching into infinity.

As CIOs, we need to start thinking seriously about redefining our roles. I've written this book to launch what I sincerely hope will be a meaningful conversation about the role of the CIO going forward, and to offer some specific suggestions for ensuring the survival of CIOs, both as individuals and as a species.

One of the most important lessons I learned as a CIO is this: Make sure that everyone knows that you are responsible and accountable. When the opportunity presents itself, step up and take on more responsibility. Don't be afraid to define your role broadly, and don't hesitate to be accountable. Let's face it: As the CIO, you're going to get blamed anyway if something goes wrong, so there's no point in trying to duck. You own IT, so act like a leader and show your pride.

Demonstrating ownership and accountability makes it less likely that someone else will try to usurp your legitimate role as the company's technology czar. The last thing you need in today's environment is some self-appointed "expert" from a business unit telling you how to run IT, or recommending which systems to purchase from which vendors. I have a simple rule for establishing boundaries: If it looks like IT, feels like IT, and smells like IT, then it *is* IT—and the CIO is responsible for it.

Reality Check

Parts of this introduction appeared originally as a guest column that I wrote last year for CIO.com. One of the interesting things about publishing an article in an online publication is that readers can respond immediately. The first response to the article was from an anonymous reader who no doubt had risen from the wrong side of his bed that morning. Nonetheless, he asked what I consider to be a fair question. I'm not quoting him exactly, but the essence of his question was this:

Why should I take advice from a guy who worked for GM?

I posted this response:

Dear Anonymous: You don't have to be a sharpshooter to take potshots at GM these days. Of course, we're all disappointed by the company's recent performance. But I can honestly say that GM's IT shop was a truly world-class operation, ahead of the curve in many significant areas. I suppose that on one level it proves that when you're the world's greatest automaker, you're judged by the cars and trucks you sell, and not by the quality of your IT. That being said,

I believe in my heart that GM will survive and emerge a stronger company.

I bring this story to your attention as a warning: There will be several stories in this book about the experiences of CIOs at companies that are not performing as well as the market would prefer them to perform. The fact that these companies are not performing up to market expectations does not mean that the knowledge acquired by their CIOs is useless or that somehow their stories are irrelevant.

I would argue the opposite. I would say, that what makes these stories so valuable, is that the people telling them are struggling, surviving, and even succeeding under extraordinarily difficult conditions.

Or let me put it another way. If these CIOs can avoid disaster and find ways to prosper in the most dire of circumstances, there can be no excuse for failure or mediocrity in less extreme situations.

I certainly would have preferred writing a happy-go-lucky book recounting the joys and pleasures of working in the IT business. And while I have tried to keep the superficial tone of this book as light as possible, the underlying message is quite serious.

IT is at a crossroads and its future is unclear. Because CIOs are hired first and foremost to run IT, their futures are equally murky. We cannot know what will happen, but we can and we must position ourselves to survive the shocks that are still ahead.

Before sitting down to write this, I watched a DVD of *Saving Private Ryan*. Tom Hanks plays Captain Miller, a schoolteacher-turned-soldier who is ordered to lead his troops on a dangerous mission during World War II. The mission succeeds, largely because the captain never stops innovating, improvising, and adapting to the unbelievably difficult circumstances.

The film paints a grim and grisly picture of war, but it's worth watching. If you are a CIO, you will find parts of it especially relevant to your career.

Additional Resources

Since I am a technology person, I naturally had to create at least two Internet-based resources to accompany this book. Please visit www.thepracticalcio.com and www. josecarloseiras.com, where you will find updated content and additional materials. The first site is intended primarily for CIOs and IT executives, and I hope that it becomes a vibrant online community for sharing ideas and news about information technology. The second site will feature recent articles and commentaries on the state of IT management worldwide. It will also provide updates on events and activities connected with the book. Ideally, both sites will provide practical information that you can use in your role as an IT executive. I look forward to meeting you online!

Chapter 1

Build a Great Team

Executive Summary

As the manager of an indispensable organization within a larger business, some of your primary responsibilities are attracting, nurturing, promoting, motivating, and preserving talent. The responsibilities to find and manage talent extend well beyond the traditional boundaries of the company to include vendors, consultants, business partners, and all the various outsourcers that IT depends upon. A deep pool of talent is a great asset and the best hedge against the uncertainties of a rough economy.

My Role Model

I grew up in Brazil, where the big game is soccer. I didn't start following basketball until recently. Now I'm a huge fan. I especially like Duke University. Okay, by now you're asking: What's this got to do with IT? Bear with me for a few more sentences, please.

About ten years ago I changed jobs, which required a move from New York to Florida. Naturally, my family and I needed to sell our house. So we listed it with a broker and pretty soon prospective buyers were traipsing through the house. Adding to the general excitement, my son had just been accepted at Duke. Whenever the Blue Devils were on TV, he had to watch.

One Saturday afternoon, a husband and wife showed up to look at the house. My son was watching Duke play either Clemson or Maryland, I forget which. The husband was a basketball fan, and he sat down to watch the game with my son.

The next thing I know, I'm watching too. I didn't understand much about the game back then, but I was struck by the demeanor of Duke's coach, Mike Krzyzewski. It seemed to me that Coach K was radiating strength, intelligence, authority, knowledge, and confidence all at the same time. What a great leader, I remember thinking.

From that day on, Coach K has been my role model. I always begin my presentations with an appropriate quote from the coach, and it usually does a good job of framing the points I'm trying to make.

I've included several quotes from Coach K in this chapter, and I hope you find them helpful and inspiring. Now that you've been adequately forewarned, here's a good one to get us started on the topic of team building:

> *When you first assemble a group, it's not a team right off the bat. It's only a collection of individuals.*
>
> —Coach K

Creating a great team is not the job of human resources (HR)—it's yours. HR can help you hire the bodies, but it's up to you to weld those bodies into an effective team. Turning a collection of individuals into a team takes time and effort—your time and effort, specifically. Team building, for the most part, is a hands-on management function. You can delegate some of the tasks required to build the team, but most of them will require your personal unwavering attention.

You start by creating an environment that values transparency and trust. Then you add talent. From these three basic ingredients you build your team.

All right, I can hear you saying: Oh, he's going all touchy-feely. Here's my response: If you can't handle the full 360 degrees of personal involvement required to lead IT in today's wild and crazy economy, maybe now isn't the right time for you to be an IT executive. Maybe you should wait for things to calm down, or maybe you should look for a job with less responsibility and less pressure.

Focus on Talent

Seasoned IT executives have been around the track enough times to understand the value of a good team in good times and bad. Many of the decisions you make about staffing your IT team will be essentially the same, whether you are building up or building down. Either way, you will be prone to making mistakes.

For example, when you are building up, there is a tendency to pick someone for a particular job because that person is available and you figure, "What the heck, how badly can that person do?" That is what happens when you become fixated with the idea of "filling seats" instead of focusing on acquiring the skills you need to accomplish your team's objectives. You really need to take the time necessary to define (or redefine) exactly what you need in terms of skills before you start thinking about an actual person to fill the seat.

In my experience, hiring people in a hurry is a classic management mistake and almost always leads to unpleasant results. You cannot hire in a hurry. When I hired talent,

I would be thinking about the available job *and* the next position that would open up.

In a down economy, you will be facing the opposite problem: You need to eliminate positions. Too often, as one of my colleagues likes to say, people are eliminated "because they are sitting in the wrong chair." As managers hurry to meet corporate downsizing objectives, they often make the same mistakes they make when they hurry to meet hiring objectives.

Unfairness aside, eliminating the wrong people will severely restrict your ability to create an IT function that is smaller, leaner, and more efficient. I suggest that you start with a clean sheet of paper. Make a list of the skills, talent, and experience IT will need to survive for the next 36 months.

You can be relatively certain that you will have less money and fewer projects. The projects you do have will be smaller in scope. What will not change is this: The enterprise will still depend, to a large extent, on IT's ability to deliver a wide range of critical services at critical times.

So I urge you to think through your staffing needs very carefully. Resist the urge to eliminate positions for the purpose of achieving short-term goals. Equally important is retaining good talent. In a time of crisis, the best performers tend to leave. But you need good people to help you survive a crisis. It will take all of your executive skills to ensure that good talent does not go out the door.

Focus on skills and competencies, not job titles. If you are facing a choice between hiring an expert and hiring someone with proven abilities in a wide range of areas, hire the generalist. Look for multi-taskers, fast learners, and good communicators.

Key IT Competencies

At this point you're probably screaming, "You keep talking about skills and competencies. But which skills and competencies are required to manage IT successfully in a rapidly changing economy?"

My short answer is this: The same skills and competencies that would be required in *any* kind of economy. As a group, your IT team should be capable of:

- Understanding the industry and the competitive landscape
- Formulating strategy
- Prioritizing and managing the IT portfolio
- Defining solutions and architecture
- Estimating project costs
- Preparing business cases
- Defining and managing requirements
- Managing programs and projects
- Managing program and project costs
- Managing run costs

If you begin with these key competencies, it is not difficult to come up with a list of essential skills that your team will need. Naturally, some people will have many or several of the skills you need and some people will have fewer. It is your job to balance the needs of the team with the skills and abilities of the individual players.

And by the way, it is also your job to make sure that the team, as a group, and the players, as individuals, are properly trained. The list of essential skills and competencies is not static—it will change as the market changes.

You cannot reasonably expect people to absorb new skills by osmosis. Sometimes you can teach them new skills directly by just talking with them, explaining what they need to know and letting them figure out the rest by themselves. Other times you can hand them a book to read.

But most of the time, you will need to arrange structured, formal training to make sure that your people acquire the new skills they will need to help you manage through difficult times. Keep in mind that 70 percent of what people learn, they learn by doing. So, don't be afraid to promote young, motivated talent. Talented people can achieve miracles, particularly when they are supported by a good team.

HR can help you find the appropriate training resources. Do not wait for HR to ask you if your people need training. Make sure that HR knows that training is one of your priorities. Be the squeaky wheel and get what you need from HR.

Send Sacred Cows to Pasture

From the IT perspective, the recent economic meltdown provided at least one benefit—there's no place for the sacred cows to hide anymore.

You know which ones I'm talking about. They're easy to spot because when you ask about why they haven't been eliminated, the usual replies sound something like, "We've always used this system and everyone is comfortable with it," or "Our requirements are unusual," or "This application addresses the unique needs of a special niche of important customers."

Some sacred cows fall into the legacy category. Others fall into the "that's not the way we do things around here" category. For example, some IT organizations will resist doing a process analysis because they've never done it before. The standard response is often something like, "We know where we want to go, so why should we spend the time and money to document where we are?"

I personally know of an IT organization that had no idea how many PCs they owned. They resisted performing an internal audit—mainly because they had never done one before.

All of these types of excuses are usually offered to cover up for past sins of laziness, arrogance, or sheer ignorance. In any event, it's time to herd up the sacred cows and send them out to pasture.

After the sacred cows have met their fate, you need to replace them with systems or processes that deliver more value at less cost. This is one of the primary ways in which you fulfill your role as an agent of change.

Never Forget, You Are an Agent of Change

I have never met a CIO who was hired to enforce the status quo. I have never interviewed for a job and been told, "We like things just the way they are, so please don't change anything. Just keep the lights on and the printers running."

Companies hire new CIOs the same way that baseball teams hire new managers. CIOs are hired to shake things up, to upset apple carts, to breathe new life into organizations that, rightly or wrongly, are perceived as underperforming or not living up to their potential.

CIOs deliver value through disruption and innovation. Any competent manager can keep the lights on and the printers running. We earned that "C" in our job title because we are considered capable of challenging the norm and replacing it with something better.

A couple of years ago, everyone was talking about the CIO's role as an enabler of transformational change. Well, it was easy to talk about transformational change when there was no compelling reason to actually accomplish it. Now there is a compelling reason. Traditional IT has become unaffordable. It's like a big old rambling house that you've got to sell so you can move into a smaller, more efficient house.

But making the move will be painful and difficult. People will have to pull their own weight, and more. That is why you need a great team—people you can trust to do the heavy lifting and not drop the boxes filled with fine china.

You are going to need people who are willing to make sacrifices, who are not afraid of change, who will not cave under pressure. They don't have to be the smartest, the most talented, or the most aggressive. They have to be people who can work together in tough situations, people with enough experience to improvise, people who are OK with the idea that the survival of the organization depends on them.

It won't be enough to have two or three people who think like this. You'll need a whole organization full of like-minded colleagues. You'll need a real team to make it through the difficult times ahead. As Coach K says, "You develop a team to achieve what one person cannot accomplish alone. All of us alone are weaker, by far, than if all of us are together."

Start at the Top

How do you encourage and reward the behaviors that will enable you to succeed as the CIO? How do you set the standards?

I've always believed that the best place to start is at the top. So one of my first tasks as CIO is establishing what I call the "IT Board."

Exhibit 1.1   The IT Board

IT	Business IT	IT Support
Operations	Sales and Marketing	Finance
Planning, Strategy, PMO, Contracts	Engineering (Product Development)	Purchasing
Architecture and Standards (Application and Infrastructure)	Manufacturing	Legal
	Logistics (Supply Chain)	HR
	Finance and HR	

Essentially, the IT Board serves as the CIO's cabinet. I select members of the board from two main constituencies: my direct reports within IT and managers from key functional areas such as finance, purchasing, HR, and legal. I then divide my direct reports into two groups: IT and Business IT. That makes a total of three groups within the board: IT, Business IT and IT Support. (See Exhibit 1.1.)

Once the board is established, I regard it as the primary representation of the company's IT management function. We hold regularly scheduled meetings (at least once a month, but sometimes more frequently depending on the circumstances) at which attendance is mandatory. There is always a formal agenda. We circulate detailed minutes of the meetings to all members of the board.

A substantial amount of time is dedicated in each meeting to organizational planning. Each member of the board presents a detailed overview of the organization that he or she manages or represents. The entire board reviews these presentations so we all know at all times where we are strong and where we need help. This is absolutely critical.

Each member of the board is required to make suggestions for improving the organizational make-up of the various components that comprise the IT function. We then discuss these suggestions as a group, and take action when necessary. This really helps us avoid nasty surprises and the ensuing panic that invariably leads to poor decisions.

Another key focus of the board is continuous improvement. Particular attention is paid to reviewing and learning from incidents and system outages. More about that later. Again, all members of the board are required to report on the status of their organizations and update the board on their activities in this area.

Cost reduction is another standing item on the board's agenda. Keeping cost reduction on the agenda means we can't avoid discussing it, reviewing it, arguing about it, and refining our strategies. It forces us to deal with new information as it surfaces and to work through issues and opportunities in a formal setting in which everyone has a voice and is expected to contribute.

Sharing information on a regular, communal basis enables everyone on the board to learn something from everyone else. It formalizes the knowledge transfer process and creates a stage on which everyone gets the opportunity to play a starring role.

Overall, however, the main difference between the IT Board and an informal group of advisors is the sense of shared responsibility. I make it very clear to everyone on the board that we alone are responsible for all the decisions affecting IT or IT-related processes.

As mentioned in the Introduction, I define IT much more broadly than many CIOs do. Remember the mantra: *If it looks like IT, feels like IT, and smells like IT, then it is IT.* So the IT Board covers a lot of territory and shoulders a lot of responsibility. Once you have joined the IT Board, there is no turning back.

When the board makes a decision, it is a group decision based on shared information, careful review, and open discussion among peers and colleagues. We do nothing in the dark or behind closed doors. We are transparent. Every important IT decision goes through the IT Board.

That means that no one can say that he or she did not know about a new system or a modification or a new operating process that affects his or her area. More importantly, it means that implementations are likely to go more smoothly (resulting in faster, better return on investment [ROI]) since the board will have already identified and dealt with many of the potential problems.

That is the real advantage of the board. It creates partnerships across the enterprise. When people feel they are partners with their peers and colleagues, they are more likely to speak up when they see a potential problem and flag it before it becomes a serious issue.

When managers stop thinking in terms of "we–them" and start thinking in terms of "us," they become much less timid and more proactive. They are less likely to run away from problems and much more willing to confront them head-on. This is the kind of support you need from your staff if you're going to succeed as the CIO in hard times.

Another advantage of the board is that it really helps you prepare for the senior management meetings that you attend as CIO. I always felt confident bringing a matter to the company's board of directors after the matter had been thoroughly reviewed and discussed by the IT Board. I knew there would be no surprises, because I knew the IT Board had already thought through every possible scenario, and I knew that the IT Board would stand behind the recommendation that I brought forward.

Find a Friend in Human Resources

It is imperative for the CIO to work closely with HR. That is why you want an HR person on your IT Board. Staffing needs are fluid, to say the least, and you want someone in HR who understands precisely what you need when you need it.

When I was the CIO at GM Europe, I was fortunate to work with Robin Watson, one of the company's best HR managers. Technically speaking, Robin worked for HR and IT, which meant she had one foot in each world. This arrangement was occasionally difficult for Robin, but it worked out great for the company.

Robin felt personally responsible to make certain that IT was staffed with top performers. Because she was a member of the IT Board, she understood the specific needs of IT. Her years of experience in HR enabled her to find the best possible candidates and to optimize the hiring process.

"HR brings certain skills to the table that can help the CIO build a great team," she says. "For example, we know how to ask questions that will reveal whether a candidate is a good learner and can adapt quickly to new situations. Since we 'get' IT, we can keep our eyes out for good candidates as they become available and bring them in sooner. We try to follow Ross Perot's advice. When he was running EDS, he said he would rather hire a musician than a technician because he knew the musician would be capable of learning."

HR can also coach the CIO on the best methods for building a successful team, says Robin. "First of all, you need to establish the goals and objectives of the team, and then build the team around those specific goals and objectives. So the key questions are: What is the team trying to accomplish? What is the team's mission? What is the team's charter? Which specific skills and competencies will you need on the team to make it successful?"

Once you've specified the team's purpose and listed the skills you need, then you can start building the team itself. "Many executives make the mistake of building their teams around people instead of around needs," says Robin. "That can be a recipe for disaster."

For example, when we're building a senior IT team, we look for experienced managers with proven track records in operational management and financial management. We also want them to have strong critical thinking skills. And they have to be good people managers, since managing people is a critical skill for IT leaders. The ability to manage people does not come easily to many IT executives, but it is an ability that you must cultivate in order to succeed.

Good communication skills—both verbal and written—are also critical skills for senior IT managers. Since IT touches every part of the enterprise, IT leaders must be ready to communicate fluently at multiple levels with multiple audiences. It's not unusual to find yourself talking to the board of directors in the morning, a committee of internal customers in the afternoon, and a group of vendors in the evening. And of course you'll be on your BlackBerry™ all day, trading e-mails with people you know, people you don't know, and people you don't want to know!

The point is that IT no longer dwells in a dark basement or behind a glass plate. IT is everywhere, which means that IT managers need to be comfortable in any kind of milieu or environment. Come to think of it, we should probably add diplomacy to the list of critical IT management skills required for a high performance team.

The High Performance Team

My friend and former colleague, Alejandro Martinez, uses the phrase "high performance team" to describe his ideal IT organization. Alejandro is the current CIO of General Motors Europe, recently promoted from managing Latin America, Africa, and the Middle East. You would think from reading the headlines that GM is suffering all over the world, but the company is still very competitive in Asia, Latin America, and Eastern Europe. That is a big chunk of the world to compete in, and that is why I believe that Alejandro's advice is worth listening to.

In any event, it is fair to ask: What exactly is a high performance team and how do I build one?

"In a high performance team, everyone knows what the team is trying to accomplish. Everyone knows the rules of engagement. Everyone is motivated. Everyone is empowered to act in ways that will ensure the success of the team's mission," says Alejandro. "The CIO's job is communicating all of this to everyone on the team."

A high performance team moves fast, excels in execution, and delivers more value to the business than a traditional IT organization. A high performance team also requires hands-on, highly visible leadership.

"No matter how technically brilliant you are, you cannot be a successful CIO in today's environment if you stay behind your desk," says Alejandro. "You need to be out in the field, you need to be seen, and you need to be available when people want to speak with you. You need to invest your time in managing your people—because your success rests on their ability to accomplish the mission."

I asked Alejandro to give me some examples in which a high performance team accomplished missions or achieved goals that would be considered beyond the reach of most traditional IT organizations. He told me two great stories, and I want to share them with you.

A Quick Start in Russia

About two years ago, GM began implementing a plan to establish a significant presence in Russia. The plan required us to move quickly and aggressively. We had a very aggressive go-to-market strategy.

This represented a huge challenge for IT because we rely largely on outsourcers and we expect them to conform to standard systems. But there were no traditional IT suppliers in Russia at this time. So we had to build the capabilities of our global suppliers from scratch.

When we selected our team, we made sure that we included people who knew how to identify and develop local resources, develop recruiting strategies, choose the right vendors, make sure the contracts were properly written, work with project managers on the vendor side, and train new suppliers and integrate them smoothly into our IT organization.

The team also drew on expertise throughout our existing IT organization; we leveraged our strengths and capabilities. For example, if the best project manager for a financial application was in the United Kingdom, he or she would take the lead on that project and work with the team until the project was completed.

This was an entirely new approach for us and it really was a tremendous stretch. Our goal was to create an IT infrastructure that would enable GM to start building cars in Russia, and there were challenges on every front.

But after 24 months, we had deployed an IT infrastructure that included financial, HR, manufacturing, supply chain management, quality, operations, purchasing, contracting, project management, and incident management—all the best practices of a traditional IT organization.

Best of all, we were able to replicate our global standardized model. So if you go into our IT shop in Russia today, it looks just like our IT shop in Canada, Brazil, or China. It was really a remarkable achievement, and it would have been impossible to accomplish without a high performance team.

Profiting from a Unique Opportunity in Brazil

About seven years ago, a change in the Brazilian tax code created an opportunity for local car buyers to legally avoid a fairly significant state sales tax when they purchased cars directly over the Internet. We were reasonably certain the tax code would be revised in the future, so if we wanted to take advantage of the opportunity, we needed to act quickly.

Avoiding the tax would shave two to three percent off the buyer's cost of a car, which amounted to a true competitive edge in some of our more cost-sensitive markets.

The problem was that we didn't have a car that we could sell effectively over the Internet without disrupting our existing distribution network. So we had to invent a new car, the Celta.

We created a new business model for building and marketing the Celta, literally from the ground up. IT was just one piece of the program. But we were a major player since IT was essential to every part of the program from design to engineering to manufacturing. And of course, we had to invent new business processes and unique business-to-consumer capabilities.

The program, which started before I became CIO of Latin America, pushed IT to the limit. Because we already had a high performance team in place, we were able to handle the additional strain and deliver the IT services necessary to make the program work.

Naturally, when our competitors discovered what we were doing, they tried to build up their Web presence and start selling cars over the Internet. But we had such a head start that they never caught up, giving GM a unique competitive advantage.

To make a long story short, we were the only car manufacturer in South America that successfully sold cars over the Internet during this period of time. We designed, built, launched, marketed, and sold the Celta before anyone could figure out what we were doing.

The Celta program was a major business success. It remains a great example of how the partnership between IT and the enterprise can accomplish magnificent results in a short span of time.

Global Team for a Global Effort

Harvey Koeppel, the former CIO of Citigroup's Global Consumer Group, told me a great story about his efforts to establish a truly global customer relationship management (CRM) system to support the bank's rapid expansion into new markets. The technical challenges were staggering. The bank had 180 million customers in 54 countries. The goal of the project was to provide customer profiles to customer representatives on demand, within 200 milliseconds. Here is how Harvey described the project:

> We called it "customering," and it went beyond the classic CRM implementation. We wanted to create a comprehensive repository of customer information—one place where we would collect, store, and process institutional knowledge about the full relationship we had with each of our customers. The system included business intelligence and analytics. It was automated and context-sensitive so the reps didn't have to scroll through all kinds of irrelevant data to find the specific information they needed to deal with an individual customer's question or problem.

The scope of the project was huge, much of the technology was relatively new and the expectations were sky high. Well, if you've ever met Harvey, you know that he is a big guy with broad shoulders. But they're not *that* broad. Nobody has shoulders broad enough for all of that responsibility.

So the first thing Harvey did was create a special team. The team had to have the right combination of technical knowledge and local knowledge, since privacy laws and business customs varied from country to country. For example, storing some specific kinds of customer information might be legal in one country, but illegal in another country.

We pulled together a team of hard-core technologists—application and process experts, as well as infrastructure and architecture experts—and some very savvy business people. We knew that we were breaking new ground, both from a technology perspective and a business perspective. Nobody had ever attempted anything like this before on such a grand scale.

The fact that we had executive sponsorship from the top was a major critical factor in our success. But the team had to get the job done.

The team was aligned around the vision and the goals of the project. The team represented the appropriate distribution of skills. There was a lot of transparency and accountability around specific aspects of the project and everyone understood that he or she had a particular role to play as a member of the team. The focus wasn't on individuals and their creative artistry—the focus was on the goal and mission that we needed to accomplish.

At its peak, there were 80 people on the team, including consultants, vendors, and other third-party suppliers. The initial deliverable was accomplished in nine months. There was a series of follow-on projects that went on for another four to five months.

Frankly, we got it done so quickly and so completely because we had put together a great team. That was the "secret" of our success.

I hope you found these stories interesting and useful. While we understand on a gut level why focusing on the team is important, it is often difficult to translate our gut feelings into practical strategies and tactics. That is why we need to dig a little deeper and really look closely at the way in which good teams are assembled.

For example, when Harvey was putting together his team at Citigroup, he looked first for people with very strong program management skills. He wanted people who could grasp the vision, decompose the business problems into a series of technical challenges, staff accordingly to address each challenge, and then orchestrate the development and implementation of practical solutions.

> *Within the team we had several sub-teams working on different aspects of the architecture. There was a business intelligence sub-team, a middleware sub-team and a SOA (service-oriented architecture), sub-team. There were sub-teams for data privacy and information security. We also had people from legal, finance, HR, operations, sales, marketing, and customer service. The team had tentacles into every department of the bank.*

In a very real sense, the team operated as a mini-department of the bank. Maybe it should have been called the Department of Transformation since it played a crucial role in the bank's evolution from a product-centric organization to a customer-centric organization.

When the team's work was complete, it was disbanded. I would like to think that at least some of the lessons learned were retained in the bank's institutional memory. This is actually an important point to remember.

When you do something terrific, write it down and let everybody know about it. That way you are sharing your knowledge and making it easier for the next generation. This is something that we tend to forget in today's hypercompetitive world. After all, if a tree falls in the forest and nobody hears it ...

Remember, Communication Holds the Team Together

My friend Alejandro is a strong believer in the hands-on management style. But for Alejandro, the term "hands-on management" means something very different from "micromanagement."

Micromanagers tell people how to do things. Hands-on managers explain the mission and then let the people working for them figure out how to get it done. Any idiot can be a micromanager. I'm sure that you've met your fair share of them.

A successful hands-on manager takes the time to understand the business vision so thoroughly that he can share it easily and fluently with others. Then the hands-on manager makes the time in his or her schedule to communicate—personally and directly—with all the members of his or her team.

So if you are the CIO, you will be spending a lot of time on the phone, on the plane, on the train, in the car—you get the picture. As Alejandro said earlier, you cannot manage IT from behind your desk. Get out there in the field and talk to your people. It won't be easy, but your success will depend upon it.

Earlier I mentioned that it is important to look for senior IT managers with good communication skills. These same skills are absolutely indispensable for CIOs managing complex IT organizations in a down economy. You simple cannot afford to have members of your team behaving unproductively—and believe me, that is exactly what will happen if you aren't out there serving as a role model.

"Communication does not always occur naturally, even among a tight-knit group of individuals," says Coach K. "Communication must be taught and practiced in order to bring everyone together as one."

Chapter 2

Proactively Establish Goals for IT

Executive Summary

Don't wait for someone to tell you what to do or you'll always be trailing the pack. In a challenging economy, it's actually easier to set realistic goals and accomplish them than it is during periods of rapid growth. Since all areas of the business are in a cost-cutting mode, now is the perfect time to simplify your IT landscape by eliminating legacy systems and redundant components. Remember, IT owns the systems, so there's no excuse for not acting swiftly when the opportunity arises to ditch a costly and inefficient legacy system and revamp or replace it with a more cost-effective alternative.

You Call the Shots

As CIO, you know your company's IT systems better than anyone. Or at least you should. Don't put yourself in a position where someone else is telling you what to do with your IT systems. That would be unfortunate. You're the boss of IT; you call the shots.

Obviously, one of your first tasks will be cutting costs. You will have to move aggressively and intelligently. Don't bother looking for low-hanging fruit. By now, most of it will be gone.

My suggestion is to divide your cost-cutting activities into three tracks. That will make the decision-making process more manageable. Remember, this is likely to be the most difficult challenge of your career. Here are the three tracks I use to "divide and conquer" my cost-cutting objectives:

1. Discretionary spending

2. Non-discretionary spending

3. Service contracts

Discretionary Spending

Here's my advice: Kill any new projects that do not contribute directly to running the business or that have a payback longer than 12 to 18 months. You will never be able to justify the cost of these projects in a down economy, so kill them now before they start putting serious holes in your budget.

Here are some likely targets: Projects that do not clearly increase revenue, such as marketing and business intelligence applications. In today's environment, there is a good chance that these types of applications are not absolutely necessary, at least not in their present forms. Kill them now, and wait for the next generation of cheaper, more effective applications before investing in them again.

Kill IT projects aimed at providing new services with doubtful benefits. Focus instead on extracting maximum utility from services you already provide. For example, when was the last time you looked hard at your corporate e-mail application? Can you figure out how to get more value from it without investing new capital?

While you are on the hunt, keep a sharp lookout for any "pet" executive projects that will not immediately benefit the bottom line. Kill any projects that have no sponsor. If no one is willing to stand up for a project, get rid of it.

Look closely at internal IT projects. Sometimes unnecessary projects can sneak in under the radar and drain funds from your budget before you even realize it.

Don't forget to eliminate the personnel running the projects that you decide to kill. Identify the top performers, move them to more important projects, and send the rest packing.

Non-Discretionary Spending

Eliminate applications and services that are not necessary for running critical business operations. Look for these applications in all the functional areas IT serves (sales, marketing, HR, finance, operations, etc.)

Think about eliminating (or drastically reducing) support for all applications, especially the ones that you plan to replace or the ones that are no longer absolutely necessary for running the business. Again, do not forget about the personnel providing support for all of these applications. Protect your top performers and let the rest go.

Explore replacing paid services and software with free alternatives such as Linux, Web mail, or Web-based office applications.

Implement IT projects that will reduce costs. Virtualization, for example, is a logical choice for the cost-conscious CIO (and who among us isn't?) since it can help you reduce power consumption and eliminate legacy hardware.

Service Contracts

This next piece of advice is simple, at least conceptually: Renegotiate all your service contracts. Remember, many of the contracts you have in place are no longer as valuable to you as they were in the past. As a result, now is the perfect time to renegotiate all of your IT contracts.

Remember two important points:

1. All contracts can be renegotiated.
2. A renegotiated contract must be a win-win for you and the supplier.

Focus your efforts on renegotiating application support and run-cost contracts. Look for ways to save *pennies* when renegotiating recurring cost contracts for services such as applications maintenance, hosting, and support. Look for ways to save *dollars* when renegotiating one-time contracts for services such as applications development and implementation.

My own personal rule of thumb is this: Always try to get two projects for the price of one.

It Pays to Be Proactive

In the introduction I mentioned that I have lived through several recessions and recoveries. As many of you remember, there was a recession at the beginning of the twenty-first century. At the time, I was working at GM. I will share with you a story about how we reduced operational costs in IT by 35 percent. The key to this success was our decision to replace an integrator. It sounds like a simple decision, but it was in fact very difficult.

Back in the mid-1990s, the company had made a decision to standardize enterprise resources planning (ERP) operations across Europe. An integrator eventually was selected and implementation of the program began. The integrator's plan was to begin with the company's smaller operations in Portugal and Spain, and then move gradually toward the company's larger operations in Germany, Belgium, and the United Kingdom.

When I arrived in 2001, the integrator had completed a major chunk of the project development at a cost of more than $100 million. Apart from the money that had already been spent, I became very concerned about the run costs. It seemed that wherever the integrator went, run costs had gone up.

I could see that operational costs—the very costs that we were trying to hold down—would skyrocket as the program was deployed in more countries. This would not be acceptable at any time, much less during a recession.

Now it is important to understand that the integrator was doing the job it had been hired to do. The real problem was that the finance department, not the IT department, had hired the integrator. The people in finance were comfortable with the integrator because they had worked with the integrator's parent company for many years. And they were afraid of assigning a project of that magnitude to another vendor that was less familiar to them.

To me the issue at hand was no longer a matter of familiarity or comfort—the project simply cost too much money.

Besides that, I believed strongly that since the project was, by any reasonable definition, an IT project, IT should have the final say in selecting the most appropriate vendor.

So we re-bid the project. The original integrator submitted a bid, but another integrator beat its price. I frankly wasn't afraid to switch vendors because I was confident that my IT team had the competence and the expertise to manage a new vendor successfully.

Within a relatively brief period of time we had achieved a 35 percent reduction in run costs and I was able to convince the company not to drop the savings to the bottom line. Instead, we applied the savings to simplify the solution and to continue the deployment of the project to the larger operations in Germany, Belgium, and the United Kingdom. That was critical to our long-term cost-reduction plan, because the greatest cost-savings from the project would be achieved at those larger operations.

It is very important to mention that we also implemented a state-of-the art disaster recovery system for this application. Our supplier decided to build two data centers in the Netherlands to support the application with the idea of providing run services for other companies. We provided the supplier with our requirements and helped the supplier build the data centers. The resulting data centers were intentionally redundant (to avoid the possibility of downtime) and the application had an extremely high level of availability.

We achieved this success because IT proactively took the reins of a major project that appeared to be heading toward a disaster and we assumed the responsibility for getting the job done properly. As I said before, *if it looks like IT, feels like IT, and smells like IT, then it is IT*—and IT is responsible for it.

Because I had assembled a great IT team, I had no doubts that we could manage a complex project that stretched across most of Western Europe.

Whenever Possible, Integrate

Let me tell you another story from my tenure at GM Europe. We acquired a significant competitor in Northern Europe and naturally, we made various efforts to achieve cost reductions through the elimination of unintentionally redundant systems.

The acquired company had its own culture and wanted to keep its IT systems separate from its new parent. But now it was a division of a global enterprise, not a freestanding entity.

Soon it became clear to me that the new division's IT costs were out of line compared to the revenue it was generating. Maybe another CIO would have let the division continue "doing its own thing," but I believed very strongly that the division's IT operations should be tightly integrated with IT operations of the enterprise. I believed this in my gut and in my mind. It turned out that I needed guts and brains to accomplish what I needed to do. One without the other would not have been enough to overcome the challenges.

Why I Am Comfortable With Numbers

Maybe at this point you are wondering, "Why is this guy looking for trouble?" I can assure you that I did not want to pick a needless fight. My actions were driven by a genuine concern about the numbers that I saw when I looked carefully at the division's financial books.

At this point, I should mention that my first job out of high school was in the accounting department of Kibon, the largest ice cream manufacturer in Brazil. I went to college at night, and worked in accounts receivable during the day. It was 1968—a time of great change all over the world.

Not long after I began working there, Kibon deployed its first computer system. I remember my boss calling me into his office and telling me that we were going to start using an "electronic brain" to help us in our work. The way he talked about it made it seem kind of scary.

My first inclination was to run out the door. My anxiety only deepened when he told me that he had signed me up to take a class in computer programming. I had heard that people who worked with these "electronic brains" went crazy and so I told my boss emphatically that I wanted no part of this new-fangled technology.

My boss, of course, convinced me to take the class. I learned the machine programming language for our Burroughs B-500. For those of you too young to remember the early days of computing, the B-500 and its various components took up an entire room. It was big and not particularly powerful. For the sake of comparison, I will guess that my iPod nano has 600 times more computing power and capacity than the B-500.

I took the class and I did well. In fact, I really enjoyed it! I enjoyed it so much that when my boss transferred me to the company's newly formed management information services group, I was delighted.

Even today, I still love to write code. And I have not forgotten my training as an accountant and financial planner. During a period of almost two years when I was working for General Foods in Spain, I managed their financial planning department when Spain was joining the European Economic Community. Those skills—programming, accounting, and financial planning—have given me the confidence and the ability to make critical judgments on a surprisingly wide range of IT issues over the years.

Back to Our Story

On its surface, the idea of combining the IT functions of the enterprise and the newly acquired division seemed absurdly logical. But the reality of the situation was more complex. I had to develop a plan and sell it to top management. After receiving management's blessing, I had to make sure the plan was implemented smoothly and effectively.

Exhibit 2.1 shows some of the arguments I used to win my case with top management.

Total Cost ($Millions—One Time)		
IT Cost	Expense	$33.7
	Capital	$5.3
	Sub-Total	$39.0
Business Cost	Expense	$5.1
Grand Total		$44.1

Total Cost By Year ($Millions)	
Year 1	$3.5
Year 2	$19.7
Year 3	$12.1
Year 4	$8.8
Grand Total	$44.1

Tangible Benefits ($Millions—Per Year)	
IT Cost Savings	$20.1
Business Cost Savings	$3.3
Total	$23.4
ROI (Weighted)	50%

Benefits Not Quantified

- Business synergies resulting from process integration
- Easier to do business with GME (Suppliers, Dealers, Employees)
- Manufacturing flexibility
- Integration with alliance partners and JV's

Exhibit 2.1 High Level Financial Summary

The financial argument was important. But it was equally important to win the hearts and minds of the division's IT team. To be perfectly honest, they had some legitimate fears about integrating their legacy systems with the newer enterprise systems. In some areas, the enterprise systems were not that good. But generally, the enterprise systems were good enough to handle the additional loads and I was certain that the trade-offs would be manageable.

The division's CIO would not buy into the program, so I had to replace him with a new CIO who believed in the program, knew the new systems, and could work smoothly with the enterprise IT team. It was important for the new CIO to build bridges from the division to the enterprise, since the enterprise IT team would be carrying heavier workloads during the transformation process and would be supporting the division after the process was completed. Their cooperation was absolutely crucial.

The new CIO played a major role in bringing people together, fostering a sense of teamwork and reducing the overall level of anxiety that people naturally experience during any time of significant change. His performance as a manager had to be virtually flawless, and fortunately for all of us, it was.

One Step at a Time

To reduce the chance of a major disruption, we agreed to move forward in a series of discrete steps, or blocks, working around a series of product launches that were critical for the success of the company. We began by replacing the division's engineering applications. Next we tackled human resources, payroll and CRM. After that we the replaced order-to-delivery and finance systems.. And finally we replaced the sales and after-sales systems. (See Exhibit 2.2.)

The results spoke for themselves. The cost of the integration program was about $44 million, spread out over four years. The program saved the company $23 million annually over roughly the same four-year period, yielding an ROI of about 50 percent.

Along with those tangible benefits, the program also generated intangible benefits. For example, it created an ongoing series of opportunities for fine-tuning and harmonizing operations across many functional areas of the enterprise.

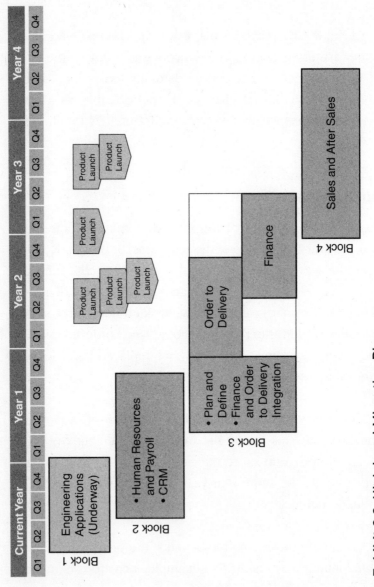

Exhibit 2.2 High Level Migration Plan

The success of the program made it easier for our dealers and suppliers to do business with us. It also made it easier for us to integrate our IT processes with the IT processes of our alliance partners and joint venture partners. Last but not least, we introduced a new level of flexibility into the division's manufacturing processes, creating efficiencies that would have been difficult or impossible to achieve if the process integration program had failed or stalled.

Our accomplishment validated my core belief that IT leadership has intrinsic value in a modern global enterprise. I am certain that if IT had not taken a leadership role and had not assumed a wider set of corporate responsibilities, the program and the benefits it engendered would not have been possible.

Chapter 3

Design the IT Strategy

Executive Summary

Even in the best of times, you could not raise capital for a business unless it had a strategic plan. Think of IT as a business and think of your company's board of directors as a group of venture capitalists. Write out a strategy for IT, share it with the board, and use that strategy as the template for everything you do.

You Were Hired to Solve a Crisis, But . . .

Despite what everyone would like you to believe, most CIOs are hired to solve a crisis or deal with a set of problems that the prior CIO could not manage. Whether the previous CIO got the boot, or simply walked away from a messy situation, the result is the same. The new CIO is expected to clean up the mess without delay.

If you are a newly hired CIO, there is no escaping the nature of your situation. You are likely to spend your first two or three months on the job dealing with tactical issues. That is the truth, so there is no point in denying it.

But—and this is a big but—the gritty reality of your situation does not remove your obligation to develop a practical strategy for IT. Nor does it relieve you from the duty of writing out a strategic plan and implementing that plan to the best of your ability.

If you are not thinking and acting strategically, then you are merely following orders and responding to pressure. The role of the CIO demands more than that. You must be a leader.

51

Unfortunately, the leadership skills required to become a great CIO are usually learned on the job. To my knowledge, they do not teach these skills in business schools. Maybe in the future they will, but for the moment, you will have to improvise as you go.

Learn from the Masters

One of my early mentors was Jim Onalfo, who is now the CIO of the New York Police Department. I have known Jim for more than three decades, and he is one of the IT industry's living legends.

I first met Jim when I was still working at Kibon in Brazil. Jim had been sent to Brazil by General Foods, Kibon's corporate parent, to oversee a major overhaul of our IT systems. In the two years he spent working with us in Brazil, he implemented 30 new applications and set up two new data centers. He really knew how to get things done, quickly and effectively.

Jim was unique because he had really taken the time to study the organization that he worked for. He absorbed the culture around him, and he learned from it. Back in the 1970s, General Foods was one of the world's leading multinational corporations. The company excelled in all the areas that market leaders are supposed to excel in: strategy, product development, marketing, manufacturing, sales, distribution, and so on.

General Foods was justly famous for packaging and marketing hugely popular consumer products such as Jell-O, Grape Nuts, Minute Rice, Sanka, Tang, and Dream Whip.

But General Foods was also particularly good at strategy. Over the years, the company had developed rigorous processes and methodologies for developing strategy. The company's focus on strategy was actually a competitive advantage, although many people did not seem to appreciate this fact.

Jim, to his everlasting credit, adopted part of that world-class strategy development process for the IT organization. "I looked at the strategic planning methodology they were using at General Foods and I mimicked it to the best of my ability," says Jim.

This brilliant piece of improvisation might not seem like such a big deal now, but I can assure you that Jim was a pioneer in applying real-world strategy development processes to IT management. Every other IT executive that I knew at the time waited for the business to tell him what to do. Jim was the exception.

His next major insight was aligning IT strategy with business strategy. Again, this probably seems like a no-brainer today, but in the 1970s and 1980s, this was revolutionary thinking.

"We would look at the business strategies of the company and ask ourselves, 'What are the implications of these strategies on IT?' Once we understood the impact, we could explain it to the business in language that everyone could understand," says Jim.

Jim's ability to render difficult IT concepts into commonly understood business terms was a tremendous asset to the IT department. When the business executives understood what we were doing, they were more likely to approve our funding requests and more likely to consider practical alternatives to their pet projects.

Jim also taught us to separate all IT projects into three buckets:

1. Strategic (growing the business)

2. Cost reducing (saving money)

3. Sustaining (keeping the lights on)

When we presented IT projects for approval or reviewed a proposed IT project from one of the business units, we always dropped them into one of the three buckets. That made it a lot easier to estimate the real value of each project that was proposed, and it made it possible to create a realistic schedule that tackled projects in order of their priority. It also made us look like we knew what we were doing, which was critical back in those days.

"When you present your arguments in the form of simple business logic, the general manager or president or CEO is much more likely to say, 'OK, now I see why I have to spend money on this project.' If you can show your boss how a project fits into the company's business strategy, you're on the right track," says Jim.

My Approach to IT Strategy

Later on I worked with Jim at General Foods headquarters in White Plains. He taught me quite a lot about developing strategy. The methodology that I learned from Jim helped me develop my own approach in the years that followed.

My approach begins with the assumption that you will have at least two meetings every year with your company's executive board. These meetings must be dedicated exclusively to IT strategy.

The purpose of the first meeting is to identify IT programs and projects that are necessary to help the company achieve its strategic goals. The purpose of the second meeting is to prioritize the IT initiatives that have been identified as critical and secure budgeting for these initiatives.

At the first meeting, you will present an overview of IT industry trends. You will also distribute relevant technical and strategic information in the form of white papers, studies, and executive reports. And you will present a competitive assessment showing the company's strengths and weaknesses relative to its competitors.

Following this general format should lay the foundation for an ongoing dialogue between the IT team and the rest of management. Encourage the members of your IT Board to meet with their counterparts throughout the company, and make sure you have a process for incorporating the insight they gain from these meetings into your strategic plan.

Your second meeting with the board will focus on prioritizing the list of critical IT projects. This will be your opportunity to lock in support and demonstrate your understanding of the overall business strategy. As Jim discovered, everything becomes much easier when you and the business are reading from the same sheet of music.

The exhibits that follow outline the basic steps of this approach. Exhibit 3.1 illustrates the process overview that I introduced previously.

Exhibit 3.2 illustrates a typical list of IT industry trends you would present to your audience. Feel free to use this as a

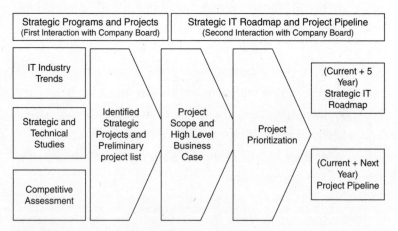

Exhibit 3.1 IT Strategy Planning Process

Domain: IT Strategic Planning
Preparer/Presenter: Dan Young

Data Source: Internal Assessment of IT Industry Trends
Data Quality: Good

Trend	Details	Applicability to Our Industry	Action	Status
Mobility	Use of mobile devices (cell phones, Blackberry) to access applications are becoming more and more relevant	Customers would like to receive status of maintenance services in their mobile devices	Start program together with dealers to explore benefits and competitive advantage of adding this functionality to dealer applications	Underway
Social Networks	Use of social networks has increased dramatically in the last 2–3 years	Possible applicability in Marketing	Marketing to conduct a study to determine how company can use social networks to promote products	New
Blogging	Blogging, where individuals use personal web site to deliver content to web community, is reaching record levels	Blogging can be used by company managers to deliver content to the web community	Corporate Communications to determine how blogging can be used to deliver company content to web community	New
Cloud Computing	Software companies are increasingly offering applications hosted in the web cloud	Cloud computing can be used to reduce IT services and IT applications cost	IT to determine if it makes sense to use cloud computing for e-mail and other IT services and applications	New

Exhibit 3.2 IT Industry Trends: Manufacturing Company Example

rough template for your own presentations. I naturally fell back on my experience in the manufacturing sector to create the example shown in the exhibit, but the template should work for any industry.

This type of trend list is important for several reasons:

- It shows that IT is pro-active in identifying opportunities to help the business.

- It demonstrates expertise on key technology issues and anticipates questions from savvy board members.

- It reminds your audience that IT knows what's going on in the outside world. If IT is perceived as too parochial, the business may try to move ahead on its own, and IT will be discredited.

- It works as a tool to educate the company board on IT trends.

- It motivates the IT group by keeping new and exciting IT trends front and center.

- It identifies sources of data and provides an assessment of the quality of the data, again showing that IT understands the importance of looking outside the enterprise for knowledge.

Exhibit 3.3 is basically a list of studies and other reference materials that are relevant to your presentation. Make sure to include links to the studies in your presentation slides so others can read them.

Study	Objective	Conclusion	Action	Status
Social Networks	Determine how the company can use social networks to promote products	...	...	...
Blogging	Determine how blogging can be used to deliver company content to web community	...	...	...
Cloud Computing	Determine feasibility of using cloud computing for e-mail and other IT services	...	...	...
...	...	...	...	...

Exhibit 3.3 Strategic and Technical Studies Template

Exhibit 3.4 is your competitive assessment. Again, since both charts refer to the manufacturing sector, you will have to customize them based on the data, information, and insight that you collect from your team and from your peers inside and outside of the enterprise.

Like the trend list in Exhibit 3.2, the competitive assessment is important for several key reasons:

- It is the result of a collaborative process involving business leaders across the enterprise and members of the company board. Ask a member of the board to present the assessment to emphasize the point that it was a team effort, and not something cooked up solely by IT.

- It helps IT understand the business and business priorities better.

Domain: Marketing and Sales
Sub-Domain: Web Presence
Domain Leader/Presenter: Jane Jones
IT Domain Leader/Preparer: John Smith

Data Source: Internal Assessment of Company and Competitors Web Sites
Data Quality: Very good

Legend ⬅ ⬍ ➡

Very Important
Important
Not Important

Strength
Basic functionality present
Weakness

Functionality	Importance to Business	Competitor A	Competitor B	Our Sites	Strategic Action	Status
Presentation of Brands and Products	⬅	⬍	⬅	⬅	Investigate use of social networks to promote product	New
Online Product Build	⬅	⬅	⬅	➡	Short-term: Add functionality to existing site. Medium to Long-term: Replace current site	Underway
Online Ordering	⬅	➡	➡	➡	Add this functionality to dealer sites to enhance competitive advantage	New
...						

Technical Assessment: Our web presence consists of several different web sites that do not provide users with a good experience. In addition the web sites are slow and not well integrated with underlying applications

Technical Action: Web 2.0 Architecture is being built. Next step is to convert current web sites to Web 2.0 technology, separate data layer from application layer, and integrate sites

Exhibit 3.4 Competitive Assessment: Manufacturing Company Example

60

- It makes the business stronger by using IT as a strategic resource to enable and support competitive initiatives.

- It allows IT to show strengths and weaknesses of existing applications.

- It identifies source of data and provides an assessment of the quality of the data.

Exhibit 3.5 is a preliminary list of strategic projects that have been identified in the various studies and assessments. It includes rough estimates of cost (provided by IT) to help the board determine if the project should remain on the list or not.

Exhibit 3.6 shows the scope of the projects you have proposed and presents a high-level business case for each project. This is a project-by-project summary of business cases showing firm estimated costs and benefits. Since the strategic planning process is conducted every year, the process will mature and the business case will become more precise and more sophisticated.

Exhibit 3.7 shows the projects in order of priority. Essentially this is a list of projects with the priority recommended by IT and agreed by the company board. The example in the exhibit shows only one domain (Marketing and Sales), but the list should include all of the company's projects.

Depending on budget constraints, an "affordability" line can be drawn anywhere in the chart. Projects below the line are not funded.

Project	Domain	Description	High-Level Cost Estimate	Status
Web 2.0 Service Architecture	IT/Marketing and Sales	Build Web 2.0 IT infrastructure to be used for all future web projects	$2M	Underway
Convert Existing Sites to Web 2.0	Marketing and Sales	Prioritize and convert existing web applications to Web 2.0 technology.	$4M	
Online Product Build	Marketing and Sales	Add basic product functionality to existing site as a short-term solution. Rewrite site using Web 2.0 technology to provide full functionality	$3.0M	Underway
Online Ordering	Marketing and Sales	Add product ordering functionality to dealer web sites. This will require a complete rewrite of dealer sites using e-commerce and Web 2.0	$1.0M $5M dealers	
Social Networks Study	Marketing and Sales	Feasibility study of using web social networks to promote products	$0.5M	
Mobility for Services	Marketing and Sales	Determine benefits and competitive advantage of using mobile devices to provide status of maintenance services to customers	$1M $2M dealers	Underway
		Total	$11.5M $6M dealers	

Exhibit 3.5 Identified Strategic Projects: Preliminary Project List

Project

Online Product Ordering

Description

Add product ordering functionality to dealer web sites. This will require a complete rewrite of dealer sites using e-commerce and Web 2.0

Scope

- Rewrite of customer-facing dealer web sites to provide real-time product configuration and pricing
- Changes to underlying engineering and pricing systems to provide required information to web sites

Dependency

Web 2.0 Services Architecture

Out-of-Scope

- Web 2.0 Services Architecture, which is a separate project
- Delivery dates. Web sites will not provide at this time promised delivery dates

Cost Item	One-Time	Recurring
Rewrite of dealer sites	$1.5M	
Changes to engineering and pricing systems	$0.8M	
Testing run cost	$.2M	
Yearly run cost		$.5M
Total	**$2.5M**	**$0.5M**

First year run cost charged to project

Benefit Item	One-Time	Recurring
Sales increase		$3.5M
Overhead/call center reduction		$.6M
...		
Total	**$4.1M**	
	$0	**$4.1M**

Payback/ROI

0.7 year

Exhibit 3.6 Project Scope and High-Level Business Case: Summary

Prio-rity	Project	Domain	Description	Cost Estimate	Payback (years)	Status
1	Web 2.0 Service Architecture	IT/Marketing and Sales	Build Web 2.0 IT infrastructure to be used for all future web projects	$2M		Underway
2	Online Product Build	Marketing and Sales	Add basic product functionality to existing site as a short-term solution. Rewrite site using Web 2.0 technology to provide full functionality	$3.0M		Underway
3	Mobility for Services	Marketing and Sales	Determine benefits and competitive advantage of using mobile devices to provide status of maintenance services to customers	$1M $2M dealers		Underway
4	Social Networks Study	Marketing and Sales	Feasibility study of using web social networks to promote products	$0.5M		
5	Convert Existing Sites to Web 2.0	Marketing and Sales	Prioritize and convert existing web applications to Web 2.0 technology.	$4M		
6	Online Ordering	Marketing and Sales	Add product ordering functionality to dealer web sites. This will require a complete rewrite of dealer sites using ecommerce and Web 2.0	$1.0M $5M dealers	0.7	
			Total	$11.5M $7M dealers		

- - - - Affordability line

Exhibit 3.7 Prioritized Project List

64

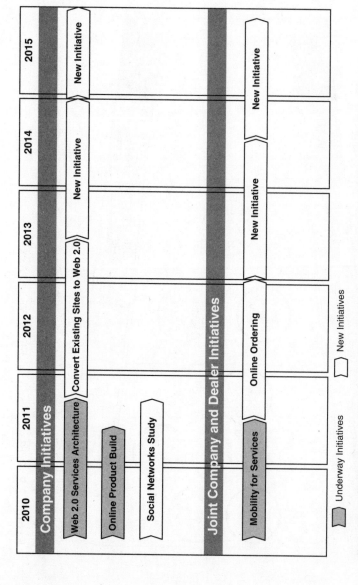

Exhibit 3.8 Strategic Initiatives Roadmap: Marketing and Sales Domain

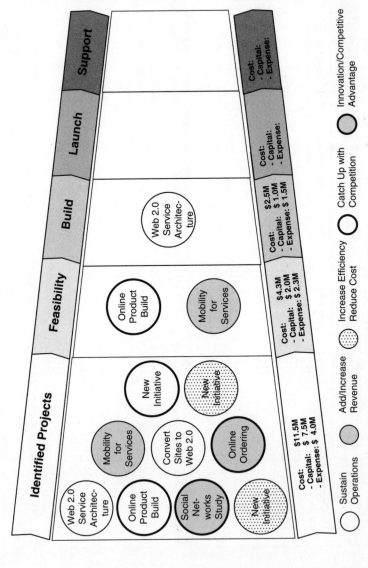

Exhibit 3.9 Project Pipeline: Fiscal Year 20XX

Identified Projects

| Feasibility | Build | Launch | Support |

Web 2.0 Service Architecture

Online Product Build

Mobility for Services

New Initiative

New Initiative

Mobility for Services

Convert Sites to Web 2.0

Online Ordering

Online Product Build

Social Networks Study

New Initiative

Cost: $11.5M
- Capital: $ 7.5M
- Expense: $ 4.0M

Cost: $4.3M
- Capital: $ 2.0M
- Expense: $ 2.3M

Cost: $2.5M
- Capital: $ 1.0M
- Expense: $ 1.5M

Cost:
- Capital:
- Expense:

Cost:
- Capital:
- Expense:

Sustain Operations

Add/Increase Revenue

Increase Efficiency Reduce Cost

Catch Up with Competition

Innovation/Competitive Advantage

Exhibit 3.8 is a project roadmap showing the current year and the next five years. Creating this long term, comprehensive view of IT initiatives is beneficial for several reasons:

- It helps engage suppliers on IT initiatives.

- It helps with short-term decisions, because it is much easier to make short-term decisions when you know where IT is heading.

- It motivates the IT team.

Remember to update the project roadmap annually. Unless something truly drastic occurs, you should not have to alter it dramatically from one year to the next.

Exhibit 3.9 shows your project pipeline for the current year and the next year. You should use it to illustrate how identified projects are funded and launched. It should be updated and presented to the company board on a quarterly basis at minimum. I would usually try to find reasons for presenting this slide to the board as frequently as possible.

As you can see, each exhibit brings you a step closer to reality. You begin with ideas and theory, and end up with a fairly solid plan.

I have used this overall process and these specific steps to develop and execute IT strategy at several global organizations, and I can tell you honestly that it works. Again, feel free to use the exhibits and concepts as the starting points for your own efforts.

Chapter 4

Hold All of Your Vendors Accountable

Executive Summary

Make certain that all vendors deliver on their promises to you. Remember, they're part of your team. Manage your relationships with them and make sure the contracts you sign reflect *your* business needs and not just the needs of your vendors.

Focus on Win-Win Scenarios

The best way to make sure that vendors keep their promises is by demonstrating that working with you will not become a zero-sum game. In other words, do not turn the relationship into a contest where someone wins and someone loses.

Make it a win-win situation in which there are no losers, only winners. Then everyone will be happy and everyone will benefit. Ideally, the relationship will continue for many years, generating profit and gain on both sides of the buyer-seller equation.

In my experience, all such happy relationships begin with strong contracts. Players on both sides need to know exactly what they're getting into and what is expected of them. Ideally, contracts should function like the rulebooks used in competitive sports. In sports, there are always disagreements and disputes. The rulebook provides a guide for resolving issues and getting on with the game.

A significant difference between you and the manager of a sports team is that in your role as the CIO, you will have to serve double duty—sometimes you will be a manager and sometimes you will be a referee. So you better make sure that your rulebook covers all the possible contingencies. If it does not, you have only yourself to blame.

Real versus Ideal

There is another huge difference between you and the manager of a sports team. In sports, there are only two teams on the field at one time—your team and the other team.

In a typical IT scenario, however, there are usually multiple vendors. It does not matter whether you are talking about a software development project or a long-term service agreement, you must assume from the onset that multiple vendors will be involved.

The contracts you negotiate with these vendors must reflect this stark reality. If it does not, you will be setting yourself up for some unpleasant surprises.

Here is a story told to me by a good friend who shall remain nameless. He was the CIO of a shipping company. One of the business units had contracted with a company that provided a beautiful automated voice response system. When customers called, the system would automatically figure out what they needed and instantly route their calls to the appropriate area of the company. This was what the vendor had promised.

This beautiful software ran on hardware provided by another vendor. That hardware required specialized software provided by yet another vendor. You can see where all this is leading, right?

In all, the business unit had to rely on ten different vendors to make its beautiful automated voice response system work. They had been caught off guard by the complexity of the system. They negotiated separate contracts with each of the ten vendors.

Now IT was called in to manage the new system. IT began rolling out the new system and at first, everything worked fine. But when the calls reached half the system's expected volume, it blew up.

Suddenly, nothing worked. The system, which had become the company's primary interface with its customers, had frozen in its tracks.

Fighting panic, the CIO began calling the vendors to find out what was going on and to get the system working again. But none of the vendors would accept responsibility for the meltdown. Each pointed fingers at the other vendors.

The CIO had to revive the company's old call center system and the company had to hire back a bunch of its call center agents to handle calls from customers. Ironically, many of these agents had been laid off when the new automated system was launched.

So what went wrong? In a word: everything. There were problems, ranging from minor to major, with each component of the solution. Considering the complexity of the solution, however, it was not surprising that unexpected problems arose. CIOs deal with software defects and hardware issues all the time.

The fatal problem was caused by the contracts—none of which had designated a lead vendor. Not only were the vendors pointing fingers, one of the software vendors was actually monitoring usage in real time and was curtailing service—without telling anyone—whenever the contract volume was exceeded. So the system was dropping calls—and no one knew why!

The contracts also did not require the vendors to perform stress tests of the entire solution before it went live. As a result, operability issues and other various bugs were discovered only after the system was up and running.

If this story made you queasy, maybe you should skip the next one. The same company also operated an automated shipping center. The center was so big that it occupied three buildings.

Basically, the shipping center was a huge sorting machine run by computers. Packages would come in one end of the machine. The packages would be scanned. Then they would be carefully sorted according to their destination. Next they would be whisked across the center by conveyor belts to planes and trucks waiting at the other end of this gigantic machine.

The company's entire business model relied on this machine to work perfectly, 24 hours a day, seven days a week, 365 days a year.

The machine, in turn, relied on a highly complex system of hardware and software solutions. All of these components had to work together seamlessly, like musicians playing in a symphonic orchestra.

One day the machine stopped working. The company's operations ground to a halt while the CIO tried to figure out which solutions had failed, why they had failed and how IT could get them fixed.

Where were the vendors? Again, they were pointing fingers. In hindsight, you can appreciate their perspective. The contracts had neither designated a lead vendor, nor spelled out clearly which vendors were responsible for making absolutely certain that the machine kept running, no matter what. Everyone had just assumed that when something went wrong, the CIO and the IT department would leap into the breach and make everything OK.

Insist on Continuous Improvement

I hope these horror stories have served their purpose. My goal in recounting them was to underscore your responsibility for holding IT vendors accountable—especially when the vendors provide services or products that are critical to your business.

Not holding these vendors accountable would expose your company to a level of risk that would be unacceptable. Not holding vendors accountable would be irresponsible. Such behavior would be unsuitable for a C-level officer of the company.

Obviously, it is a lot easier to manage vendors effectively after you have negotiated good contracts with them. But good contracts are only the beginning of the process.

You must also demand continuous improvement from your vendors. Benchmarks for continuous improvement can be written into contracts, but it will be your responsibility as the CIO to make sure that your vendors actually deliver on these promises.

At this point, it would be natural to ask: How do you make sure that continuous improvement is woven into the fabric of your IT operations? How do you make sure that continuous improvement becomes a fact of life and not just a catchphrase?

Let me offer some suggestions. At the twice-monthly meetings of your IT Board (I hope that you have taken my earlier advice and established an IT Board), review all incidents and problems that occurred in the past 15 days. Now that you have made a list of all the recent issues, schedule face-to-face meetings with each vendor associated with an issue.

Tell the vendors that you are going to ask them to explain not only what happened and how they fixed the problem, but also what they are doing to ensure that the problem does not occur again.

Bring the vendors in to meet with your IT Board. Make sure to include their presentations on the meeting's official agenda. Get them to agree on a series of action items for remedying the problems. Make sure those steps are included in the official minutes of the meeting. That way, nobody forgets and you have a record of what was agreed to.

Remember the story of the CIO and the automated voice response system? He eventually managed to get it fixed—and then it broke down again! Apparently, he had not made it clear to the vendors that he wanted more than just a quick fix. What he really wanted was for them to improve their processes so the system would not keep breaking down.

Until he sat down with each of the vendors and explained exactly what he wanted—a program of continuous improvement that would identify and eliminate problems before they became serious—the vendors just kept doing what they had been doing in the past.

This might seem blindingly obvious, but the simple truth of the IT universe is that if you do not ask for something, you will not get it.

Contract or No Contract, Get What You Need

Sometimes you have a good contract and sometimes you do not. The CIO at the shipping company was new and he had not been involved with negotiating the vendor contracts. From a contractual standpoint, he was on shaky ground. But he knew that from a moral and ethical standpoint, he had the high ground. And he knew that the vendors needed his company's money.

Now the CIO needed to show the vendors what he was made of. He needed to demonstrate his mettle and express his resolve in no uncertain terms.

So he told the vendors that he wanted to audit their processes. That got their attention. Grudgingly, they agreed. Some of the vendors allowed the CIO's people to conduct the audit, others insisted that a third party conduct the audit. Either way was fine with the CIO because he got what he wanted:

- Greater visibility into the vendors' internal processes.

- More attention from the vendors.

- Objective data and information that he could feed into the IT department's continuous improvement process.

I am not recommending that you immediately start dashing off e-mails to your vendors announcing your intentions to audit their processes. In my opinion, requesting an audit should be the last step of a process in which you escalate problems up a vendor's chain of command.

Let me tell you a true story that happened when I was the CIO of GM Europe. As most of you probably know, GM acquired EDS and then later sold it. But many people within the GM organization still regarded EDS as though it were a part of the company, and many people at EDS still considered themselves to be part of GM. Sometimes, these misperceptions made it easier for us to do business with EDS, and sometimes they made it more difficult.

In this case, they made it more difficult. We had a situation in which a critical IT system that was managed by EDS began experiencing major outages all over Europe. It turned out that too many people had access to the system and were making changes to the directories. As a result, it kept blowing up. So we asked EDS to reduce the number of people who were allowed to access the system and make changes.

When the problems continued, we asked them to restrict the number of authorized users to an even smaller group. But the problems continued. Now it was my turn to blow up.

I told them that I wanted to audit their internal processes to find out exactly what was going on. They refused. They reminded me that they were no longer a division of GM. As an independent company, they would not submit to an audit by a customer. I told them, okay, so don't call it an audit. Call it an assessment. And you can do it yourself and report the results to me. As long as we get to the bottom of this issue, I will be satisfied.

They conducted their own audit and found out that people were sharing passwords. They discovered that no one really knew how many people were using the system and making changes. That is why it kept crashing. Once they understood this, they were able to make the necessary changes to prevent the problem from occurring again. At the end of the day, everyone benefited from the audit.

No vendor likes being told that you want to audit their processes. They all react emotionally, and that is understandable. An audit is not something that you request lightly or based on a whim. It will make many people angry. An audit costs money and can take weeks to complete.

But I can tell you this based on my experiences: When an audit is over and done, the vendor always thanks me, because it helps his company to become more efficient and provide better service to their customers.

The moral here is that sometimes you must insist on an audit (or an assessment) to get to the bottom of an issue. But you must keep in mind that the audit should result in a win-win situation that generates benefits for you and the vendor.

Internal IT Suppliers

Sometimes the "vendor" will be another part of your company. For example, when I was the CIO at DHL Express US, the IT function was split into two organizations, a "demand side" representing the IT needs of the company's various lines of business, and a "supply side" consisting of all the various IT processes themselves.

DHL was not unique in having an arrangement like this. Dividing IT into "supply" and "demand" sides had been a fashionable trend several years ago, and many large organizations followed what appeared at the time to be a logical strategy for managing complex IT operations in swiftly changing global markets.

The problem with this kind of organizational arrangement is that it has to be carefully managed or the two sides can wind up competing instead of collaborating. This next story illustrates my point.

About six months after I took the job at DHL, the company experienced a major outage in one of its data centers. My boss told me that he wanted a full report on the outage within ten business days. In other words, I had to conduct an audit of our own IT department.

I hired a consulting firm that I trusted to perform what amounted to a root cause analysis of the problem. There had actually been seven different incidents leading up to the major outage, and we wanted to find out what these incidents had in common.

The consultants reviewed our internal records, sent out questionnaires, and interviewed dozens of people at various levels of the IT organization.

To keep things simple, we set up a template to summarize our findings (see Exhibit 4.1).

Exhibit 4.1 Root Causes of Incidents and Outages

	People Issues	Process Issues	Technology Issues
Incident 1			
Incident 2			
Incident 3			
Incident 4			
Incident 5			
Incident 6			
Incident 7			

The inter-relationships between the people, process, and technology root causes were then identified and documented using classic "fishbone" diagrams. It did not take long for a clear pattern to emerge.

The IT staff was talented and experienced. The technology itself was more than adequate. It turned out that most of the problems leading up to the outage originated from process issues.

For example, we did not really know how well our IT systems were performing because of the way we measured uptime. Instead of measuring uptime from the user's perspective, we had been measuring the uptime of individual components within the system. We knew, for instance, that our customer relationship management (CRM) application was up 99.9 percent of the time and that our enterprise resource planning (ERP) solution was up 99.89 percent of the time.

What we did not measure—and therefore did not know—was how well the entire integrated system was running from the perspective of the users. We were not measuring, for instance, how often the customer reps did not have access to data they needed to deal effectively with customer issues or how often account managers were locked out of the system when they needed to look up the status of an important account.

The audit also showed us that because of the supply side–demand side structure of the IT department, many people on the IT staff were not entirely certain who they reported to or what their mission was. This was a huge issue.

The audit also revealed that an "us versus them" mentality had taken hold on both sides of the IT organization. Neither side was willing to collaborate fully with the other because each side felt the need to protect its own turf. You do not need an advanced degree in management to see that this kind of arrangement can be a recipe for disaster.

When you have an IT organization that is split into supply and demand sides, it is absolutely crucial for everyone to understand their roles and their responsibilities. It is also imperative to have a clear set of rules establishing hand-off points within all processes and sub-processes.

Ultimately, we identified specific action items pertaining to people, process, and technology that were required to address the root causes of the incidents and outages. These were further categorized into immediate, mid-term, and long-term activities, and cross-referenced to existing IT initiatives to ensure integration and avoid conflicts as well as redundancies.

The watchword here is clarity. Only when the rules, the roles, and the responsibilities are made manifestly clear can the two sides of a split organization work well together. When there is no clarity or limited clarity, the two sides will inevitably clash—and the enterprise you are supposed to support will suffer.

Escalate Problems Quickly and Decisively

Whenever you have an issue, it is very important that you escalate the issue to the appropriate level while it is still fresh. It may sound simplistic, but you have to teach your internal teams and your vendors to pass problems up the chain.

Why do you have to teach them? Because most IT people love to solve problems on their own. The trickier the issue, the greater the challenge and the greater the personal sense of achievement when the issue is resolved. So they will resist the urge to ask for help—it's their nature.

Unfortunately, the instinct to "do it yourself" can lead to more problems. For starters, the longer you delay asking for help, the longer the issue is likely to continue. If it's 3 A.M. and a file is hanging up the system handling inbound calls, the lone operator on duty will focus on figuring out how to get the file un-hung. Working on the issue for a couple of hours in the dead of night probably makes the operator feel good, but meanwhile your call center in another time zone might have missed 200 inbound calls.

So there is an immediate cost associated with the operator trying to resolve the issue—now the operator's attention is diverted and who knows what could be happening in other parts of the system.

The other problem is that if the operator is lucky enough to resolve the issue, there is a good chance that no one will know about it—because now it is no longer an issue.

This can be a real problem, especially when the operator resolves the issue with the IT equivalent of a band aid. Quick fixes can be impressive, but they rarely address underlying issues—and if you have underlying issues, you need to know about them sooner rather than later.

So you need to train everyone on your team to think like a team player and share problems as soon as they arise. If the team leader gives the operator the green light to go ahead and work on the issue, that's fine. But no one should feel empowered to function as a lone wolf—that kind of behavior is neither smart nor practical.

Depending on the severity of the issue, the CIO or some other senior executive in IT should communicate directly with the vendor associated with the issue.

For example, if you are the CIO and you are experiencing issues with a business-critical IT solution, by all means call the vendor's chief executive officer (CEO) on the phone. Escalate serious issues to the highest possible rank. Sometimes it can be a waste of time to talk with anyone except the top dog.

Here is my advice: During your contract negotiations, tell the CEOs of your vendor organizations that you will call them directly if there are serious problems. Explain to the CEOs that these calls, if necessary, will benefit their organizations by providing important feedback that can be used to improve the products and services they offer.

Leaping Into the Fray

It does not matter whether you are purchasing new technology or upgrading technology that you already own, your objective as the CIO is always same: maximizing the return on your spending.

But how do you extract the maximum value from your IT investments, especially when many of the decisions leading up to those investments were made before you arrived or without your full participation?

In many situations, you will just have to take a deep breath and jump into the battle—even if it was not your battle to begin with.

My friend and former GM colleague Beth Kirkpatrick tells the story of how a series of avoidable IT blunders cost the company millions during the early days of its OnStar service.

OnStar is an in-vehicle system that provides security, communications, and diagnostics capabilities. For a variety of plausible reasons, OnStar was launched as a separate business within GM. Part of the rationale, I believe, stemmed from fears that GM's vast bureaucracy would make it difficult for a new business like OnStar to achieve its objectives within a reasonable timeframe. Another likely part of the rationale might have been GM's hope that if OnStar proved successful, it could be sold as a service to other automakers and perhaps, with luck, emerge as the industry standard. Or it could have been that GM was hoping to spin the venture off as a separate business at some point in the future. I really do not know the exact reason.

In any event, OnStar operated with a large degree of autonomy. It hired a vendor to provide the system's emergency response services. I will let Beth tell you the rest of the story in her own words:

GM and the vendor negotiated downtime for maintenance. But the contract did not require the vendor to provide a redundant system that would keep the system running during the maintenance periods. OnStar had apparently assumed that because it was an emergency system, the vendor would provide 100 percent uptime.

As a result, OnStar had to go back to the vendor and contract for a redundant system. It turned out to be a very expensive mistake for GM.

Yes, the vendor should have asked more questions and challenged some of the original assumptions. And yes, OnStar should have seen the potential for a problem and flagged it before it became a big issue. But OnStar had been empowered to act on its own, without IT oversight and outside of the normal GM procurement system. Bottom line, OnStar did not have the expertise required to negotiate the contract it needed to offer uninterrupted 24/7 service.

From my perspective, this story offers several important lessons.

- If you have access to internal resources that will help you negotiate a good contract, use those resources. If you do not have access to internal resources, find someone outside the company who can help you.

- Always make sure that you ask the vendor one simple question: "Does this contract contain everything I need to achieve my objectives?" If the vendor cannot give you a straightforward answer, hold off on signing the contract. If the contract has already been signed, explain your problem to the vendor and do everything in your power to renegotiate the parts of the contract that are creating problems.

Chapter 5

Before Negotiating, Do Your Homework

Executive Summary

Very few CIOs relish the prospect of negotiating contracts with suppliers. Even fewer of them enjoy renegotiating contracts. But in a difficult economy, sometimes you need to bite the bullet, call a supplier and say, "You know, this deal just isn't working." That's when you need all your ducks in a row, because renegotiating a contract requires more than courage—you need to know precisely what you're trying to achieve and be ready to offer alternatives.

No Two Suppliers Are Alike

Bob Turner, the CEO of Smart Software Deals LLC, is an expert at negotiating IT supplier contracts. So I asked him to tell me what every CIO needs to know before they begin negotiating with a supplier.

"To start off, the CIO needs to understand that supplier. Every supplier has its own way of structuring deals, pricing software and services, and negotiating contract terms and conditions with their customers. So the first thing that a CIO needs to do is to figure out how each supplier approaches the table," says Bob.

Long before the negotiations begin, the CIO has to decide if the relationship with the supplier will be strategic or tactical. The CIO must look in the mirror and ask, "How important is this supplier to my organization? Will I be counting on this supplier to help the enterprise achieve its strategic business goals, or am I only hiring this supplier to fix a short-term problem?"

After the CIO has identified the supplier as strategic or tactical, the CIO can move to the next step, which is deciding what type of agreement to pursue. Then the CIO can negotiate accordingly.

Now it is always important to remember that the supplier's sales team will want you to sign an agreement that is based on the supplier's standard terms and conditions. This makes sense from the supplier's perspective, because the supplier has spent a lot of time and energy determining precisely which terms and conditions will minimize their responsibility and yield the highest profits over the life of the contract.

As the CIO, your job is pushing back and getting the supplier to focus on your business objectives.

"Frankly, most CIOs are not great negotiators," says Bob. "For example, let's say the CIO is planning to use a supplier's software for five years. He also knows that the business is likely to grow over that period of time, and that he will need more licenses. It would be foolish for the CIO to negotiate a contract that doesn't reflect his knowledge, but often that's exactly what happens."

In a situation like the one Bob is describing, a really sharp CIO will negotiate a five-year deal that addresses the expected growth—and does not include the annual price increases that the supplier will initially demand. "If the CIO commits today to growth, then the supplier should commit to pricing the additional software at current prices," says Bob. "Otherwise, why would anyone assume the risk and commit to the additional software before they have identified an actual need for it?"

There are many advantages to this kind of deal. The CIO will be happy because he has cost predictability for multiple years, he is saving his company a significant amount of money over a five-year period of time, and he has more flexible licensing terms and conditions. And the supplier will be happy because:

- The supplier has the CIO locked into a long-term contract that will grow in value.

- The supplier is keeping out the competition.

- The supplier now knows for certain that the CIO sees their relationship as a strategic partnership.

- The supplier can accurately forecast the committed revenue for multiple years.

How Did You *Know* That?

It is also imperative for the CIO to understand how the supplier recognizes revenue and how its sales teams are compensated. Most software companies and their sales teams measure success by totaling up how much revenue they booked from selling new software and adding new licenses over the last 12 months.

If you are a CIO, you know how expensive these new licenses can be. Obviously, the sales team will be trying to structure a deal that puts the most money in their pockets. So they will do everything they can to get you to buy more licenses for their software.

When you understand this, you can respond with a practical counteroffer: Tell them you want a multi-year contract and that you're willing to commit to buying some additional software, upgrades, and professional services from them. In exchange for those commitments, you expect the supplier to discount the price of new software and additional licenses you buy over the life of the contract.

These are exactly the kinds of win-win deals the CIO should be seeking. In truth, however, many CIOs do not have the resources or the experience required to negotiate intelligently with suppliers.

That is another good reason why you need to build a great IT team to support you. If you put together a team with depth and experience, chances are good that someone on your team will know enough about a particular supplier to give you an edge in your negotiations.

For example, did you know that:

- Some large vendors will almost always agree to discount the cost of maintenance and support services by 30 percent if you commit to buying new software from them?

- A few major companies that license software on an annual subscription basis will offer perpetual licensing models if you press them hard enough?

- That a well-known global supplier offers incredibly steep discounts on maintenance and new licenses if you commit to a multi-year contract?

- The best time to negotiate software contracts is at the end of the supplier's fiscal quarter or year, when salespeople are desperate to fill their quotas?

Even if you do not know which vendor has a history of caving in when really pressed, you should expect someone on your team to know—or to know someone who knows.

Remember at the end of *Monty Python and the Holy Grail* when the remaining knight turns to King Arthur and says in wonderment, "How did you *know* that?"

That's how your suppliers should feel about you. They should be wondering, "How did he *know* that?"

Read That Contract Again Before You Renew It

Avoid falling into the common trap of automatically renewing agreements with suppliers. Putting it bluntly, renewing a contract without reviewing it is a sign of laziness and poor judgment.

"You'd be surprised how many people just automatically renew their licenses at list price," says Bob Turner. "Why? Because it's easier and more convenient than doing some research and finding out how much money you could save. Sometimes people renew an agreement because they don't really understand all the terminology and they feel intimidated. But you have to do the financial analysis and work hard to reduce the total cost of ownership of the software over the term of the agreement."

I agree wholeheartedly with Bob. Take the time to find out how important the supplier is to your business. You might be overestimating the value of the software or services you are buying. You might be overestimating how much you really need all of the bells and whistles you agreed to when the contract was originally signed.

Remember, we are operating in a highly dynamic landscape. If you negotiated a contract two or three years ago, the chances are good that the contract is already obsolete in many respects. So you need to go back and re-evaluate the contract's value to your business.

Do not be afraid to demand an explanation of any terms in the contract that you do not explicitly understand. When it comes to ambiguous terms like "cloud computing," "network performance," and "maintenance reinstatement," everyone has their own definition. It is likely that your definition does not match the supplier's definition.

Bob recommends assembling a checklist of ambiguous terms, and then finding out how the supplier defines these terms. You might be shocked at the difference between how you define a term and how the supplier defines the same term.

Make Sure Your Suppliers Follow *Your* Checklist

One of the first things they teach new pilots is to use a checklist. Pilots use checklists to make sure they do not accidentally forget important tasks—such as lowering the landing gear or closing all the cabin doors.

Suppliers should also use checklists when dealing with their customers. But make sure they use the checklists that you give them.

Make a checklist of everything that is important to your organization and share that checklist with your vendors. Explain to them that you expect them to follow *your* checklist, and that your checklist is likely to change over time.

The critical point here is that the checklist serves as a practical tool for keeping your priorities front and center in the supplier's mind. In my experience, I have found that you must use any and every tool at your disposal to keep your suppliers focused on your needs.

You can also use the checklist as a basis for renegotiating contracts. The key is writing down your priorities, and sharing them with the supplier. Making a checklist does not involve a lot of work, but it pays off big dividends—especially when you are negotiating or renegotiating a contract.

"It's really just a matter of sitting down, looking carefully at the new environment around you and then making sure that you negotiate a deal so that it makes sense in this environment," says Bob. "Maybe you need less software than you did last year, or maybe you need more. Maybe you need the ability to move software from site to site, something most vendors won't allow you to do unless you specifically negotiate it into the contract."

The good news is that most suppliers are aware of the pressures that you are facing, and most of them will agree to revisit aspects of a contract that no longer make sense in the current economy.

Do not be shy about reinforcing the idea of win-win scenarios when you are talking with suppliers. For example, if you need to reduce the scale of a project, the supplier can probably scale back the size of the development team required to complete the project. If you need to scale back the scope of a service agreement, the supplier can reduce costs on his side by reducing headcount or shifting resources.

If you and the supplier are committed to making the deal work for both of you, there is a good chance that a better deal will emerge. Remember that the supplier will probably want to keep you as a customer.

"All suppliers know that if they are not cooperative now, they will be looked upon less favorably by their customers when the economy turns around," says Bob.

The practical CIO understands this and uses it as a bargaining chip. The practical CIO also accepts responsibility for carefully reviewing all contracts and when necessary, renegotiating them.

Sometimes Regional Makes More Sense Than Global

We have all heard so much about the need for global IT strategies that sometimes I think we lose sight of the advantages of regional strategies.

I was reminded of this during a recent conversation with Marco Stefanini. Marco is a fellow Brazilian and the CEO of Stefanini IT Solutions, a global IT consulting firm. Marco believes that in some circumstances, it is more practical to choose regional suppliers over global suppliers.

Even though global contracts and global deals are all the rage these days, such contracts tend to be relatively inflexible and they can prove difficult to manage. Depending on the country, globally-contracted services can be more costly than services you obtain on a local or regional basis.

Marco recommends finding a middle ground so that you do not find yourself trapped in an "all or nothing" type of situation. Take the time to ask yourself which services should be handled locally and which services should be handled globally. Do not just blindly follow corporate policy and always choose global suppliers. Make a thoughtful appraisal of the local or regional situation, and base your contracts on the practical needs of the organization.

Regional contracts in Marco's view, can be the middle ground. Even though you will have one contract per region, they are still manageable, easier to implement and result in lower costs and greater efficiencies for the enterprise. Marco also notes that when a regional strategy proves particularly effective, it can be extended to other regions. Maybe one of the takeaways here is that in a turbulent global economy, regional strategies can give you more flexibility and fewer headaches than global strategies.

This appears to be the emerging consensus of CIOs in many parts of Asia, where IT needs are growing so rapidly that global contracting strategies cannot be updated quickly enough to keep pace with the changing business landscape. Sometimes you have to accept the idea that bigger is not always better, especially when bigger means slower.

Chapter 6

Manage Contracts, Don't Just Sign Them

Executive Summary

Negotiating a good contract can be a burdensome chore. But managing a contract is where the real works starts. Just because you have a signed contract with a service provider does not mean that you can put your feet up on your desk and relax. Business conditions can change, rendering some conditions in the contract meaningless. A shift in business strategy might require you to seek new terms. Nothing is chiseled into stone, no matter what the lawyers tell you. Most of all, a contract does not guarantee performance. It is your job to make sure the provider delivers.

The Seed Crystal

Always remember: The quality of your relationship with a supplier is shaped and defined by the contract that you and the supplier sign. So obviously you want to have comprehensive, well-written contracts with all of your suppliers.

If you work at a large company, you will have plenty of resources within the company supporting your efforts to negotiate good contracts. You will have help from legal, purchasing, finance, and other departments.

But in the final analysis, the contracts you sign are a reflection of your personality. If you are tough, honest, and fair, you will negotiate contracts that are tough, honest, and fair. If you are weak, disingenuous, and trying to create an unfair advantage, the contracts you negotiate will come back to haunt you and your organization for a long, long time.

A True Story

When I was hired as the CIO of General Motors Latin America, one of my first responsibilities was signing a ten-year contract with EDS for IT support services.

The contract was huge—hundreds of pages—and very complicated. Worse, it had been drafted 18 months earlier. From my perspective, it was already obsolete.

I also did not want to waste several weeks sorting through the details of a contract that someone else had drafted. I needed to focus on the business challenges facing GM.

So I called a meeting with the EDS people. And I told them I was signing the contract, but that I was going to do what made sense for GM whether it was in the contract or not.

EDS was no longer a part of GM at this time. But EDS was highly dependent on its former corporate parent for revenue, so I knew that I had the upper hand. Nevertheless, it was hardly an ideal way of doing business and it took months for me to get everything straightened out properly.

The moral of this story is that you, the CIO, must control the contract process. You can hire specialists and consultants to help you, but you must not simply delegate the contract process to the supplier. That would be a serious mistake.

It is *Never* a One-Shot Deal

Almost every contract you will sign as the CIO is a contract involving some kind of service that will be provided to you over a specified period of time. You are never simply purchasing something that can be delivered in a box. Even if you are purchasing a specific piece of hardware or software, you are also purchasing a relationship with the supplier. Some of the relationships will be brief; some will last for years. That is the way it works in the IT universe.

You should regard the contract with a supplier as a map of the relationship between you and the supplier. Just because you have a map does not mean that you cannot get lost. If you plan to drive the relationship—and I strongly urge you to do so—then you must learn how to read that map. Study it hard, and look for places where you are likely to lose your way, and figure out alternate routes for arriving at your destination.

Managing Contracts Like a Pro

Airline pilots are taught to do more than just fly their planes; they are taught to practice good cockpit management. As the CIO, you should practice good contract management.

So far, we have touched on this subject only cursorily. Now I would like to take a deeper dive. To begin, I would like to introduce my former colleague and good friend, Claude Marais. Claude is partner and managing director of governance services, at TPI, Inc., a global advisory firm that specializes in outsourcing, outsourcing management, offshoring, and shared services. Believe me, Claude and his buddies know how to negotiate a contract. Perhaps even more importantly, they know how to *manage* a contract.

But it would be better if I let Claude explain in his own words.

There are two distinct parts of every contract process. The first part is the negotiation, and that represents about five percent of the time you're going to spend on the contract. You will spend the remaining 95 percent of your time managing that contract. The best CIOs start putting together a strong governance organization well before the contract is finalized and they have their governance processes ready to start working on the day the contract is signed. We know from historical data that if you do not have a strong governance organization in place, you will probably lose somewhere between 15 and 30 percent of the contract's value.

Like Claude, I have known many CIOs who rushed into a contract with a vendor, thought they got a great deal, and then realized they had no plan for managing the contract. This is not a good way for doing business.

Part of the problem is that too many CIOs are still thinking like IT managers instead of thinking like IT *resource* managers. This is not a surprising phenomenon. Most CIOs are experts in technology. They are comfortable with technology and they know how to make it work.

Now the business is asking them to do something different. The business is looking for a result or an outcome. But a lot of what the business wants from IT can no longer be achieved within the traditional boundaries of IT. So now you have to go outside the organization to get it done.

For many CIOs, this feels like a stretch; it does not feel natural. They have spent their careers wrestling with technology, only to discover a new and more dangerous challenge: wrestling with suppliers.

"You have to move yourself away from the idea of managing an internal IT organization and move towards the idea of managing a diverse group of IT service providers. For most CIOs, this can be a difficult transition. But you really have no other choice in today's environment," says Claude.

Claude estimates that only a small percentage of the CIO population has fully come to grips with this new reality.

I still hear CIOs telling me, "What's the big deal? I contracted with the supplier for server hosting. We told them what we want, we put the service levels in place, and now all I have to do is pay the invoice at the end of every month." When I hear stuff like this I can only shake my head. Because I know what's likely to happen next. The vendor won't perform to the service levels in the contract. Or the vendor will measure its performance to make it appear as though it is meeting the contract, but the CIO's company won't be getting the service it needs to achieve its business goal. At the end of the month, the CIO will get a huge invoice from the supplier and instead of going through it line by line, he'll just pay it. Meanwhile the company is missing its targets. And the CIO won't even know—until maybe it's too late.

Claude's story makes an excellent point. Just because you have a contract in place does not automatically mean that you can sit back and relax. The truth is that your service levels should be aligned to the goals and objectives of the business.

When you write the contract, you try to align the service levels and the business needs as accurately as possible.

But as we all know, the business never stands still. It keeps moving. Priorities can change from moment to moment, depending on market conditions, pricing, demand, interest rates, and a thousand other external pressures. Everything is subject to change, and the business naturally expects IT to respond immediately.

That means that you need to have a way of adjusting the service levels in your contracts with IT suppliers. But you also need to have a process in place for knowing which service levels should be changed and precisely who is authorized to make those changes.

You also need to ask yourself if you have too many or too few service levels in your contracts. Most contracts have too many, which makes it even more difficult for the CIO to figure out if the vendor is performing well or not.

Remember also that service levels cost you money. If you have 100 or 200 service levels in a contract and you're only looking at 10 of them, you are wasting money.

Claude likes to say that service levels drive behavior. I agree. The CIO is responsible for making certain that the contracted service levels are driving the behaviors and the outcomes required to achieve the goals and objectives of the business.

Do not allow your service levels to stagnate or to wander off course—because eventually your business will follow them.

If you suddenly realize that the service levels are taking you somewhere other than your intended destination, sound the alarm. Tell the vendor, document the issues, and follow up to make sure the issues are resolved swiftly.

All of this should be part of your governance process. In my experience, good governance enables you to prioritize service levels and manage them accordingly. It also enables you to evaluate service levels on a regular basis and adjust them when necessary.

Good governance is also a timesaver because it reduces the chaos around you. You can use that extra time to review the invoices from your vendors more closely. Those invoices can be long, but I urge you to go through them carefully. Claude tells me that he automatically assumes that most invoices contain errors. So make sure that you are paying for the services you actually received and not paying for someone else's mistakes. Resist the urge to just sign the invoice and send it along to accounts payable.

Do Not Focus Solely on Vendor Performance

Many IT organizations use vendor performance as a tool for assessing their own performance. This is a big mistake. Vendor performance is a critical measurement, but it is not the only measurement. You also need to measure how well your governance processes are performing.

"If you're only looking at how well your service providers are doing, you're not seeing the full picture," says Claude. "You also need to look at how well your governance processes are working. You need to know how well—or how poorly—you are managing your vendors. That's absolutely critical."

Advanced IT organizations use dashboards to track the performance of the service providers and to keep an eye on their governance processes. A really sharp CIO will insist on having the capability to see all aspects of the IT picture on a single screen. Conceptually this is not difficult to achieve, but from a practical perspective, it can be challenging to consolidate all of the information you need and present it graphically on one screen with drilldown capabilities. That being said, it is certainly worth the effort.

Claude uses Exhibit 6.1 to illustrate the types of information required to manage vendor performance and governance as a unified process:

As Exhibit 6.1 suggests, you should be looking at four basic types of information:

1. Performance management

2. Financial management

3. Relationship management

4. Contract management

Exhibit 6.1 Four Disciplines of Service Management and Governance
Source: Copyright © 2009, Technology Partners International, Inc. All rights reserved.

Each of these basic types is really a discipline unto itself, but you cannot get a sense of the big picture unless you can look at all four of them together.

Keeping track of all these performance measures is not merely an exercise—it is a key part of your fiduciary responsibility as a C-level officer in the company. You need to know if you are getting full value from the contracts you sign. Value leakage can be expensive, especially in big contracts.

You also need to know if the vendor is actually delivering the discounts you were promised when you signed the contract. This is important, because the vendor is not necessarily going to track this information for you. The same goes for performance credits, earnbacks, and critical milestones—you need to keep track of them. As mentioned earlier, invoice management is also crucial. You cannot simply assume that a service provider's invoices accurately reflect the services you are receiving. You need to track the vendor's performance on a very granular level and make sure that you only pay for what you actually receive.

The average CIO, according to Claude, does not keep a close eye on these measures. "As a result, they really don't know whether or not they're getting the services they contracted for," Claude says.

Exhibit 6.2 is an example of a consolidated dashboard that enables the CIO to manage both IT providers and IT governance processes:

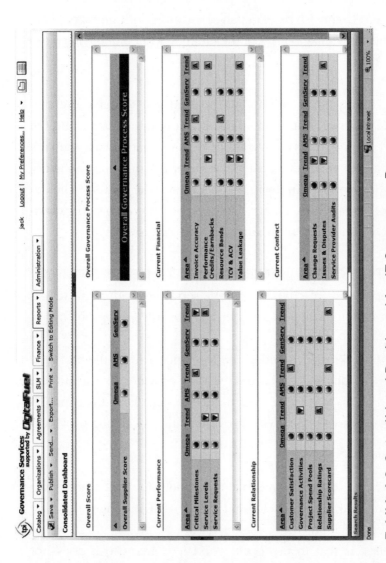

Exhibit 6.2 Consolidated Dashboard for IT Governance Processes

Source: Copyright © 2009, Technology Partners International, Inc. All rights reserved.

119

The Price of Ignorance

Being ignorant can make you look foolish and harm your career. It can also be expensive, since vendors are more likely to take advantage of you if they think you are not paying close attention.

Not paying attention can also lead you to make unfortunate mistakes that wind up hurting your organization and the service provider's organization. Here is what I mean: In many instances, the CIO realizes that his or her organization is not getting good value from a service provider and switches to another provider. Lo and behold, the CIO has a bad experience with the new provider. Can you guess why?

If the CIO's organization does not have the governance processes in place to manage its service providers, switching from one provider to another will not solve the problem.

"If the service provider's performance is really the problem, then go out and find a new service provider. But if the real problem is that the IT organization doesn't have the capabilities to manage its service providers, then switching providers isn't going to help," says Claude.

One recent trend has been to divide up work among two or more vendors, the idea being that if they feel they are in competition, they will try harder to please you. My gut feeling is that this is not a good idea because it does not address the root problem. Claude compares this approach to polygamy.

"If the relationship is poor, a multi-supplier strategy won't work. Hiring a second service provider to solve a problem is like marrying a second spouse if your marriage isn't working," says Claude. "If you can't get along with one spouse, what makes you think you will get along better with two?"

Structure Contracts to Make Your Life Easier

This is fundamental: You must structure your contracts so they can be managed efficiently. Too many CIOs make the mistake of signing contracts without considering deeply whether those contracts will be easy or difficult to manage.

Remember, service providers strive to create contracts that are complex, opaque, and ambiguous. Your job as CIO is to sign contracts that are simple, transparent, and unambiguous.

The easiest way to accomplish this is by sticking to a consistent structure for all of your contracts. The more all of your contracts look and feel the same, the easier it will be to manage them after they've been signed. For instance, when service levels are the same for the same category of applications across the board, it will be far easier for you and your team to manage those service levels.

Every exception written into the contract makes it harder for you to manage that contract. Contracts are not works of literature; they are frameworks for holding people accountable. I am sure that lawyers would disagree with this view, but lawyers are not responsible for running IT organizations.

It is also important for contracts to be structured so that basic terms do not have to be renegotiated to accommodate new statements of work. The idea here is that you do not want to be put in a situation where you have to renegotiate the contract every time a small change is required. Both parties to the contract have to agree in advance over which parts of the contract are inviolable and which parts are flexible.

You also have to agree on who is empowered to make changes and who is not. For example, if you have a global agreement, you do not want somebody in Brazil changing the contract in such a way that it adversely affects your operations in Germany. I have seen this happen, so it is not as far-fetched as you might imagine.

Seek Outside Help when Necessary

A lot of CIOs think they are great negotiators and try to do all the heavy lifting by themselves. But negotiations are only a small part of the contract process. I believe that managing the contract after it has been signed is the truly important part. After all, you are going to spend months negotiating a contract, and then years managing the contract.

If you are spending huge amounts of time negotiating contracts, I have two suggestions:

1. Stick to a basic format; contract negotiation is not an exercise in creativity. When it comes to contracts, consistency is your friend.

2. Hire an outside resource to help you write the contract and manage it. Nowadays you can even outsource many of your governance processes.

Managing contracts is all about measurement and discipline. Figure out which metrics are critical, and make sure you keep a close eye on them throughout the life of the contract.

Eyeball to Eyeball

In Chapter 3, I introduced you to Jim Onalfo, the CIO of the New York City Police Department. As I mentioned, I met Jim when I worked at General Foods and he was one of my first real mentors. Jim is a very sweet guy. But he can also be very tough when he is trying to protect the interests of the people he works for.

Jim was the CIO at General Foods International when the company's parent, Philip Morris, decided to combine the operations of its General Foods and Kraft subsidiaries in Europe, Asia, and Latin America—40 countries in total. Here is the story in Jim's words.

Basically, every country had a General Foods company and a Kraft company. So in each country we had two of everything: two sales systems, two general ledgers, etc. We obviously didn't need two sets of everything. As CIO, my job was integrating all these international operations as quickly as possible.

I arranged meetings between my CEO, Jack Keenan, and a top executive at IBM, the vendor we had hired to integrate all these systems. I sat them together in a room. Then I said to the executive, "I want you to look Mr. Keenan in the eye and make your personal commitment to him that every single country will get your best support and that we'll have no problems implementing everything necessary to make this project successful."

The IBM executive looked Jack in the eye and said, "Mr. Keenan, you have my personal word. I guarantee you that we'll get it done."

Then, good to his word, he spoke personally to his subordinates in each of the countries where we needed to integrate our operations, and he got their *personal commitments that everything would go smoothly. He also promised to personally monitor their progress and to let us know if there were any problems.*

You know what? There were no problems. Anywhere. We combined two huge global businesses with separate operations in 40 countries into one unified global enterprise. And we saved an enormous amount of money by doing so.

Back in the early 1990s, Jim's experience at General Foods was relatively uncommon. In today's environment, you never know when you might be called upon to handle a chore of similar proportions. If you find yourself in a comparable situation, I suggest that you follow Jim's advice.

When I have a major project, I sit down with the vendor's CEO and I get his personal commitment—eyeball to eyeball—that his company will do the best work and there will be no screwups. Nothing gets signed until I have his personal commitment. That's important.

What about In-Sourcing?

Most of our discussion about contracting has assumed that you are outsourcing a substantial amount of your IT operations. It might seem fair to ask, "What about IT shops that in-source most of their operations?"

My answer to that is simple: Almost all of the principles that apply to managing external resources apply equally well to managing internal resources.

For example, you can set service levels and write performance agreements with internal teams in basically the same way that you would with external providers. There is no law that prevents you from holding internal teams accountable and responsible for achieving specific goals and objectives. Written agreements might not be considered the norm at some IT shops, but as the CIO you can introduce these concepts and then use your influence to make sure they stick.

Strategies and tactics for managing internal IT resources could easily fill a whole book. Suffice it to say that it takes the same level of skill and commitment to manage internal resources effectively as it does to manage external resources effectively.

Chapter 7

Work With the Business

Executive Summary

The business values results. If you cannot deliver results, the business has no need for you. Once you understand what the business needs in terms of results, you can align IT operations to help the business deliver those results. Work with the business, not for the business.

IT's Unique Perspective: Worth More Than All the Software in the World . . .

Manjit Singh began his career at Procter & Gamble (P&G), a company built on the belief that continuous reinvention can be a sustainable competitive advantage. Some might argue that P&G is really a technology company that has become extremely adept at marketing consumer packaged goods. If that is true, then P&G deserves extra praise for visualizing the future of business and taking many of the right steps to position itself for success in a highly volatile global economy.

Like other P&G alumni, Manjit discovered that many of the lessons he learned at P&G can be applied universally. He is currently the CIO at Chiquita Brands International, where the relationships between IT and the company's various functional units have been formalized into what I would describe as a real business process.

Manjit was able to accomplish this because he truly believes that IT functions optimally when it partners with the business as an equal. Because he is relatively young, he does not remember the days when the IT department was considered a mysterious "black box" run by geeks in the basement. As a result, he tends to see the relationships between IT and other parts of the enterprise in very practical terms.

"IT touches everything, which gives us a unique end-to-end view of the whole enterprise," says Manjit. "Our unique vantage point is a genuine asset that we bring to the table. It can be especially valuable when strategy is being discussed, because it gives IT the credibility to steer conversations in a positive direction and prevent misalignments that could hurt the business."

For example, when Chiquita's supply chain group proposed a change in sourcing to benefit the company's European business, IT noted that the change would be disruptive to some of the company's North American operations.

"We actually brought all the groups together to figure out an optimal solution that would meet the needs of the European business without having a negative impact on the North American operations," says Manjit. "We came up with a workable plan that helped the company without creating disruptions. Afterwards, several people remarked to me that they had not seen the potential problems when the initial plan was developed, and that they were surprised that they hadn't thought up the solution by themselves!"

This story illustrates perfectly the "new" role of IT in the modern enterprise. Instead of merely serving the enterprise in a subordinate role, IT now brings insight, knowledge, and practical solutions to the table. As Manjit observes, IT's uniquely global view of the enterprise makes it an indis-pensable ally. In turbulent times, when business models are transformed continuously to keep pace with sudden shifts in rapidly changing markets, smart companies see IT as a strategic partner.

"Whenever someone tells me that IT is a thankless job, I think of all the moments when IT really made a difference. It's satisfying to see that people on the business side are now recognizing the added value that IT provides," says Manjit. "Most important, people understand that IT should be at the table whenever strategy is discussed."

Formalize a Process for Joining the Discussion

Of course, these elevated relationships between IT and the business do not materialize out of thin air. You need to develop and nurture them. It also helps to have a formal process for ensuring that IT is not inadvertently left out when strategy is being planned.

"If the IT organization is positioned correctly, none of these strategy conversations should occur unless IT is at the table," says Manjit. "Whenever the business contemplates changes in strategy or changes in process, you have to make sure that IT is there from the beginning of the conversation."

So how does the CIO accomplish this? "First, IT needs to be perceived and accepted as a credible business partner. Second, IT needs to have an organizational structure that keeps it aligned with all of the other business structures in the enterprise. Then you assign senior-level representatives from IT—we call them 'business unit liaisons'—to meet regularly with leaders, managers, and executives at the various business units. Basically, you are pairing up a senior IT person with a senior business person. The idea here is that whenever business teams are meeting to talk about strategy or operations, IT is always there and always participating as an equal."

Processing Insight

The insight gathered at these meetings and from one-to-one conversations with business unit leaders can be incredibly valuable, so you need a system for collecting and processing it. Manjit's system works like this.

> *I ask all of my senior people to put together a quarterly summary of the initiatives and projects they are involved with. We distribute the information from those summaries broadly across the organization.*

> *Then on a monthly basis we have a leadership meeting for all of our IT managers, including our business unit liaisons and our infrastructure folks. The purpose of this monthly meeting is sharing knowledge. Everyone is encouraged to stand up and talk about what's going on in their area. That's one of the ways we make sure that everyone knows what's going on all over the enterprise.*

I want to draw your attention to Manjit's decision to include the infrastructure managers in the monthly informational meetings. In the same way that it is critical for the business to make sure that IT is involved in its strategy planning sessions, it is critical for the CIO to make sure that the infrastructure team is represented in IT planning sessions.

"We used to joke about how the business dreams up new ideas and throws them over the wall to the infrastructure team," says Manjit. "That is a really bad way to manage IT resources. You need to have your infrastructure people involved in the conversation as early as possible so they don't get blindsided."

For instance, it is not uncommon for an IT manager to meet with a business team and agree to provide some service or capability that he or she in good faith believes can be provided. And it is not uncommon for that IT manager to find out afterward that in reality, IT does not have the resources to provide that service or capability.

These kinds of lapses are natural and understandable. But that does not mean they are acceptable. They can be avoided by involving representatives from the infrastructure team in strategy sessions. It makes sense to include them, because they really know better than anyone what IT can and cannot do.

It is easy for a business-facing IT manager to promise the business that IT can get an application up and running in four months. But if it turns out that it will really take eight months just to get the infrastructure ready, then IT will look bad, the manager will lose credibility and worse, the business will lose whatever advantage it was hoping to achieve. "It's better to involve infrastructure in the conversation from the beginning," says Manjit.

I can tell you from my own experience that the infrastructure team can also provide pleasant surprises. Sometimes you agree to provide a new service to the business and you assume that IT will have to purchase a fancy new application. Then you find out from the infrastructure team that you already have a similar application in your IT inventory, and that with a little bit of tweaking, the older application will work just as well as the newer one. Then you feel like a hero!

"A good CIO knows how to leverage the legacy footprint," says Manjit. "Even if it's only a short-term step towards accomplishing a longer-term strategy, it demonstrates the IT organization's ability to meet changing business needs without breaking the bank."

As mentioned at the beginning of this chapter, I was struck by how Manjit's prior experience at P&G helped prepare him for his role as the CIO of a multinational enterprise competing successfully in an unusually turbulent global economy. When asked about the value of his background, he offered this answer.

I think that consumer packaged goods companies tend to move in faster cycles. Innovation and new product development take place over months, not years. Something is always changing; something new is always being created. There is always a sense of experimentation. You have to be agile because you're moving at such a fast pace. I think that if you are accustomed to a faster cycle of innovation, it makes it easier to work in an environment where everything is constantly changing.

It Takes Two to Tango

Working with the business is a two-way street. So far, I have focused on collaborative strategies from the perspective of the CIO. Now I think it makes sense to hear from the business side.

Steve Marenakos is a senior vice president of annuities at financial services giant Prudential. Like many enlightened executives, he sees the relationship between IT and the business evolving away from the traditional "us versus them" and becoming much more of a partnership. This evolution, he notes, is part of a wider trend.

"We're seeing greater collaboration across the entire enterprise. Collaboration has become normal for us as we align the operations of many different functions to achieve our strategic goals," Steve says. "I think we're probably ahead of the curve in this respect, but in two or three years I think that all companies will be focusing more on collaboration. I don't see how you can stay competitive if you don't."

"One of the best ways to ensure tighter alignment between IT and the business is to bring the CIO to national sales meetings," Steve says. "It seems like a simple thing, but it's important for the CIO to hear the sales reps talking about their experiences and talking about the challenges they face when they're out there selling. The CIO picks up critical knowledge at these meetings that can be used to improve the collaboration between IT and the business. That's a big advantage for us."

In addition to attending sales meetings, the CIO oversees a formal process that systematizes relationships between IT and the business. "We have various managers, directors, and VPs within the IT organization who are designated as business relationship managers or BRMs. They have regular meetings with the business units so they understand where those businesses are going, what their challenges are and what they need," Steve explains. "The businesses develop relationships with specific individuals in IT, people they know and trust."

There is also a planning group that is responsible for gathering and analyzing the information collected by the BRMs. "We have a finite set of resources and we're always trying to figure out the optimal way to allocate those resources. The information from the BRMs is very helpful for making decisions about where to shift resources so we can get the most value from them," Steve says.

As a result of these processes, the business units feel closely attached to IT. That sense of attachment makes it easier to reach decisions that make sense for both the business and IT. It also makes it easier to align IT operations with business strategy. At a complex and highly competitive financial services company like Prudential, keeping operations aligned with strategy is critical.

The BRMs also help top management at Prudential identify emerging trends before the competition. "For example, we noticed that all of our departments were looking for a certain type of data. That gave us a heads-up about the kind of information systems we would need down the road," Steve says. "Now the IT organization can do a much better job of making sure that it has the people, processes, and technology required to deliver the information that the businesses will need to stay competitive."

IT's ability to spot subtle changes that might signal larger shifts in market conditions will become increasingly important as more companies discard long-term strategic planning in favor of shorter-term planning. IT is uniquely positioned to deliver the kind of agility required to achieve short-term goals in rapidly changing markets, making it an ideal partner to the business in times such as these.

"In the past, the business would come to IT and say, 'This is what we want.' But the business didn't really understand all the possibilities offered by the technology. And IT didn't understand what the business really needed," Steve reflects. "Now IT understands the problem. Instead of just being an order-taker, IT can say, 'Well, here's a better solution that's cheaper and faster and more effective.' That's the level of collaborative partnership you strive for."

The New Model For Collaboration

Ashlee Aldridge might be the new model for collaboration between IT and the business. Ashlee is CIO *and* senior vice president for direct sales at West Marine, the world's largest retailer of boating supplies. West Marine, which began in 1968 as a one-man mail order business operating from a garage, now has 375 stores in 38 states, Puerto Rico, and Canada. In addition to its retail stores and wholesale divisions, the company serves boaters in more than 150 countries worldwide through its direct sales segment, which includes the Internet and call center channels.

That means there are a lot of moving parts to keep track of, and IT plays a key role in making sure that all those various parts mesh together smoothly. At the same time, IT is responsible for helping the business stay ahead of the competition.

"We have to strike a balance between supporting the business and driving the business," says Ashlee. "Finding that balance can be challenging, particularly in the retail industry, because companies tend to get stuck in the rut of 'this is how we've always done it' and so they can be resistant to change."

IT, however, can be tempted to propose new and exciting solutions that might not actually help the business. That is why it is so important for IT to understand the processes and goals of the business.

"When you are the CIO, you have to absolutely understand the business so you can determine whether or not a new technology will in fact affect the business in a positive way," says Ashlee. "Some new technologies might be fun to have, but if they are not needed by the business they most likely would not generate a return. Other new technologies, however, could actually yield improved results by reducing costs, increasing productivity, or providing a better customer experience. Those technologies and projects should be pursued. But it's hard to tell without first understanding how the business works and how the business goes about the job of achieving its goals."

From my perspective, Ashlee's dual role as a technology executive *and* a sales executive provides her with a unique vantage point. In some respects, I think that Ashlee represents the future of IT as a hybrid function that stands *with* the business and *apart* from the business simultaneously. The advantage of a situation like this is that IT cannot stray too far from the business mission, since the CIO's goals encompass operational and strategic objectives.

I am sure there might be downsides to such an arrangement, but I think that West Marine is probably on the right track. Time will tell.

Sometimes There Are No Common Solutions

My friend Kevin Wale is president and managing director of GM's China Group. GM counts on him to grow the automotive business in China, and he counts on the CIOs working for him to deliver the technology solutions required to keep the various components of the business running. In a sense, he and his CIOs face a challenge that is the opposite of the one I faced in Europe.

At GM Europe, I was trying to find common technology solutions and a common technology framework that would work for all the business units in Western Europe, a mature market. Kevin, however, must find technology solutions that work for many different entities that have been brought together to create an end-to-end supply chain for what is essentially a brand new market.

"We're in a very interesting situation in China, where we have eight different joint ventures and they're all at different stages of the technology curve," says Kevin. "So the real objective is getting the right technology solution for each business and making sure you have the right cost-solution for that technology."

For example, the GM business in China that makes Buicks and Chevrolets requires a more robust set of technology solutions than the GM business that makes small commercial vehicles.

"For our Buick and Chevrolet operations, we need great technology solutions," says Kevin. "But we don't need high-cost applications to make our mini-vehicles. They have a very simple design and they require a simple manufacturing process. So we don't want to burden that business with high technology costs."

GM is also counting on its expertise and experience in telematics (the technology behind OnStar) to establish a long-term competitive advantage in the Asian market. But making OnStar work effectively in China requires another set of advanced technology solutions, adding additional layers of complexity to the challenges facing Kevin and his team.

"Figuring out your real technology needs is a constant battle," says Kevin. "It's easier for the business people to develop separate business strategies than it is for the technology people to develop separate technology strategies. But you have to find the appropriate technology solutions that will enable the businesses to achieve their objectives. You can't simply put a solution in place and tell everyone it's going to work great here because it worked great somewhere else. That's how you wind up with a white elephant."

In China and other developing markets, a major responsibility of the CIO is discovering and championing alternative solutions that might yield better results than solutions that would be considered appropriate in other parts of the world.

"CIOs must act as referees and make the difficult judgment calls about technology," says Kevin. "CIOs have to understand the business and know what kind of technology is available so they can recommend the best solution. Then—and this is incredibly important—they have to be capable of convincing people in the business that they have made the right decision and found the right technology. That's the hard part, that's the challenge."

Chapter 8

Manage and Market the IT brand

Executive Summary

IT is a product and like any other product, it cannot speak for itself. That is where you, the CIO, come in. You must put a face on IT, you must explain to the world what IT does and how it creates value. In other words, you must sell IT. But before you can sell IT, you must learn how to market IT. To the amusement of your colleagues in the marketing department, you are likely to discover that marketing a complicated product such as IT is harder than it looks.

Telling the IT Story

Unless you have been stranded on a desert island for the past 80 years, you must have absorbed some basic understanding about marketing. Even if you have never taken a business course in college, you are doubtlessly aware of the significant role that marketing plays in modern societies. It does not matter whether you are living in a society that is based on capitalism, communism, socialism, or totalitarianism—marketing is an inescapable fact of daily life.

Most successful marketing strategies are built around a simple concept—the brand. Your brand defines what you are and what you have to offer. Your brand tells your story. Ideally, your brand inspires trust and confidence. It makes people want to keep coming back to you for more.

Your brand creates a sense of familiarity. It reduces the fear that most people instinctively feel when they confront something that is new or different. Your brand makes it easier for you to accomplish your objectives, especially when you are an agent of change.

As the CIO, you are responsible for managing the IT brand. Please take a few minutes to think hard about your IT brand. What does it represent? What are the attributes that people associate with your IT brand? How do all the various services and products that you offer fit into the overall framework of the IT brand? Does IT present its offerings and relate with users in a consistent manner across the enterprise?

On the surface, these might seem like simple questions. But they get to the heart of the CIO's most difficult challenge—selling IT to an audience that often has outrageously high expectations and exceedingly limited patience forscrew ups.

Obviously, you will not be able to inspire the trust of this audience unless you are delivering the basic IT services they expect on a consistent basis. That is non-negotiable.

But after you have established IT as a trusted provider of basic services, you need to leverage that confidence into something that goes beyond "Okay, I trust you," and creates the foundation for the kind of partnerships that are necessary for growing the business in today's economy.

Managing the IT brand is an essential part of this levering process. The perceived value of the IT brand is the equity that you bring to the table. It empowers you to move ahead to the next level—assuming, of course, that you play your cards properly.

Branding Must Be Consistent With Reality

My friend Tony Scott knows a thing or two about managing the IT brand. We worked together at GM. Later he moved on to the Walt Disney Company. Now he is the CIO and a corporate vice president at Microsoft. All three of those companies place heavy emphasis on branding and brand management, so perhaps it is not surprising that Tony strongly supports the concept of managing the IT brand.

"It is absolutely important to manage the IT brand. Working at companies with strong consumer brands has really helped me appreciate the value of a strong IT brand," says Tony. "The branding process can be a very helpful part of your IT strategy because it forces you to ask difficult questions, such as 'What does our IT organization stand for?' Are we all about low cost? High reliability? Innovative delivery? It's hard to be all of those things, so you have to carefully determine what you can and cannot do."

Asking and answering those types of questions helps the IT organization establish a credible brand identity.

"The IT brand and the IT strategy should be consistent. The customer experience should reinforce the branding," says Tony. "If the branding and the experience don't match up, something won't ring true and your efforts will be wasted."

Hopefully, the IT brand will evoke strongly positive emotional responses among your customers—partly because you will have carefully crafted a messaging strategy that supports your brand strategy and partly because your customers will have had genuinely positive experiences with IT.

At Disney, for example, the IT organization's tagline was "Putting the Magic in IT." The tagline was a little bit like Dumbo's magic feather. By itself, it had little value. But the tagline was consistent with reality, and it reinforced the belief that IT supported and understood Disney's corporate mission.

Three Steps in the Right Direction

Tony's prior experience also taught him the basic tactical steps required to develop an IT brand strategy.

"Step One is taking a critical look in the mirror. You need to be honest with yourself about assessing the strengths and weaknesses of your IT organization," says Tony. "Then you should validate your observations by seeking input from your customers. Find out from them if your self-assessment was too harsh or too gentle. Ask them if the assessment hit the right points. Find out if something important was overlooked."

Step Two is sitting down and listing the IT organization's goals and objectives. Basically you are asking yourself, "What are we trying to accomplish? Are we on the right path? What do we aspire to achieve?" Hopefully you already have an IT strategy in place, so this step will be easy.

Step Three essentially consists of combining what you learned in steps one and two to create a comprehensive

Exhibit 8.1   IT Assessment Grid Template

Short-term objectives	Strengths
Long-term goals	Weaknesses

list of the IT organization's strengths, weaknesses, goals, and objectives. I suggest mapping this information onto a grid, so it will be easier to see at a glance (see Exhibit 8.1).

The grid serves as the reality check for your IT brand strategy. Your goals and objectives are your drivers; your strengths and weaknesses are your constraints.

For example, if one of IT's goals is empowering the business to respond effectively to sudden changes in the market, then your brand strategy should reflect this—but only if your organization can really deliver on this goal.

Brand Identity

Your brand identity is the face you put on your IT organization, and it flows from your brand strategy. Your brand identity is supported by the messaging you create and distribute to your customers.

Referring to the example above, your messaging would likely emphasize agility, flexibility, speed, and business savvy. Your tagline might be "Enabling agility in changing markets" or words to that effect.

All of your messaging should include the tagline, and every communication from IT should reinforce the notion that when a speedy response is essential, IT will be there and get the job done right.

Marketing the IT Brand

After you have your IT brand strategy and your IT brand identity in place, your can actually market the IT brand across the width, breadth, and depth of the extended modern enterprise.

Based on my own experiences and the experiences of the CIOs interviewed for this book, I submit to you that marketing IT is one of the modern CIO's primary responsibilities.

Now I realize that many of you, especially if your background is mostly technical, will probably recoil when you hear the term "marketing IT." Even my friend Tony Scott initially bristled at the concept. Here's what he said.

I'm actually a little suspicious about the idea of marketing IT, at least in the old-fashioned sense of the word "marketing." I've seen IT departments launch internal marketing campaigns where they try to show everyone how valuable they are, and all I can say is that kind of approach usually doesn't work.

Here's an approach that I prefer: Ask your customers to tell you how IT is helping them. Ask them why IT is valuable to them. Find out from your customers how IT contributes to their success.

At Microsoft, IT has a system for gathering and analyzing this kind of insight. Again, I will let Tony explain how it works.

We start with a list of items that we call "conditions of satisfaction." We sit down annually with our internal customer groups and update this list to keep it relevant. We also meet quarterly to discuss whether we need to make modifications to the list, based on what's happening around us.

Next we have a comprehensive scorecard that includes objective and subjective measures of IT performance and value delivery.

We also conduct satisfaction surveys. We make sure to ask the same questions consistently, which enables us to establish good baselines and to measure how well we are doing quarter over quarter, and year over year.

The combination of these three activities gives us a very honest and useful assessment of IT. It shows us where the value is and how well that value is being delivered.

This kind of systematic approach to gathering customer feedback is essential. It helps you maintain the integrity of your IT brand and provides you with an early warning when your strategy is veering off track. It also ensures that your marketing messages will be received by an appreciative audience that already feels a sense of partnership with the IT organization.

Marketing the IT Portfolio

A well-executed marketing strategy can provide very tangible business benefits for the IT organization. For example, I am sure that as a CIO you have experienced this type of scenario: A vendor pitches a new software solution to a business unit director. The director then pitches the solution to you. You poke around and discover that the IT organization already owns a similar solution. Then you curse the vendor and the director for wasting your time.

Worse still—and I have witnessed this—the company actually purchases an application or solution that it already owns. In a global organization with multiple operating units, these types of snafus are not uncommon. But they are almost always expensive.

In truth, however, when something like this occurs, the fault is yours. It is your responsibility to make sure that all of your internal customers know what is included in your IT portfolio.

In a perfect world, the CIO would market the various services and products of IT the same way that a brand manager at General Foods would market a line of consumer products to an audience of housewives back in the 1970s.

Remember, brand management is a discipline that enables you to present a portfolio of products and services consistently and coherently within an overall framework. Brand management focuses attention on the key attributes of the products, services, programs, or ideas that you are marketing to your audience.

As the CIO, your audience is everyone and anyone who uses or comes in contact with any of the company's IT assets. In addition to company employees, your audience includes suppliers, consultants, business partners, external customers, investors, analysts, academics, journalists, and hundreds of other interested parties.

I would argue that you owe them an explanation of what you offer. For internal customers, you can produce glossy brochures describing all of the applications, solutions, and systems in the company's IT portfolio. Or you can build a web portal that catalogues all the services and products offered by IT, along with contact information for the IT teams responsible for those services and products.

For external customers and other stakeholders, you can dedicate a part of your company's public web site to listing the IT resources that are publicly available. You can even include links to third-party web sites with additional information that might be useful.

Publishing this kind of information, whether online or in print, is a powerful form of marketing. You are providing useful information to an audience that has a genuine interest in understanding more about the products and services you offer.

You are also creating demand. The more your customers know about the products and services you offer, the more likely they are to use them. Higher utilization usually translates into higher return on investment (ROI), and you wind up looking like a hero.

Turn Consistency into a Discipline

I suggested earlier that brand management is really an exercise in consistency applied across a broad portfolio of product and service offerings. In a sense, brand management is similar to the efforts of global CIOs who strive to replace "legacy spaghetti" with standard IT platforms functioning seamlessly across multiple business units. As CIOs, we sometimes refer to this glorified vision of a unified, fully integrated IT delivery system as "a single version of the truth." Experienced marketers might simply call it "IT brand management."

At least that is my interpretation. Google™ the term "brand management" and you will find plenty of interesting material on the subject, starting from the "invention" of brand management by Neil H. McElroy at Procter & Gamble in 1931 right up until today.

Anything you read on the topic, however, will circle back to the idea of consistency sooner or later. Consistency is the secret of brand management. Consistency is what makes brand management an absolutely crucial piece of the CIO's IT strategy, especially in an era of consolidation and reorganization.

Today's global enterprises are like coral reefs—they are composed of many individual entities. When these entities are grouped together following a merger, acquisition, or some other form of consolidation, they do not automatically get along. In fact, they often grind against each other so furiously that the merger or consolidation is abandoned.

Each of these entities comes fully equipped with its own functions such as sales, marketing, human resources (HR), finance, and IT. For the modern CIO, melding formerly independent IT operations into a single cohesive organization can be a supremely difficult chore. It is rarely a smooth process. There are usually high levels of anxiety and mistrust to overcome, since everyone in IT will fear that jobs will vanish, projects will be canceled, departments will be relocated, and so on.

But here is where the discipline of brand management can really help you. If you already have the people and processes in place to deliver a consistent message that reinforces your brand identity, it will be far easier for you to rebuild trust, overcome fear, and encourage the spirit of collaboration necessary to move past the immediate pain and get on with the task of growing the business.

Mansour Zadeh, the global CIO of Smithfield Foods, exemplifies the kind of executive leadership required in today's business environment. In the eight years that Mansour has worked at Smithfield, the company has grown significantly through mergers and acquisitions (M&As)—18 of them, to be precise. That is a lot of M&A activity. And as you can imagine, each of those 18 deals left a fresh series of challenges on the doorstep of IT.

Many of the companies operating under the Smithfield corporate banner had been fierce rivals. Now these formerly independent companies had to stop competing and act together as one big team. As the head of IT, Mansour played a key role in helping them adjust to this new reality.

"An extremely important part of my mission has been establishing a high level of trust, teamwork, and collaboration among these former competitors," says Mansour. "We needed to convey a sense of community across all of our operating companies, and across all of the functional areas within those companies."

As you can see, his mandate extended beyond the traditional boundaries of IT. To me, this is a great example of how a smart company can leverage the reach of IT to affect change throughout the enterprise. After all, IT touches every department and functional area in the company. So it makes perfect sense for IT to play a leadership role in integrating business processes across a global enterprise.

Brand Management is Not Rocket Science

The idea for managing IT as a brand did not occur to me in a blazing flash of insight. In retrospect, I realize that the idea must have taken root during one of the many long meetings I attended as a senior IT executive at General Foods.

I remember being somewhat irked because we would spend minutes discussing the IT budget, and hours discussing various marketing programs. At one meeting, I was asked to speed up my presentation so there would be enough time for us to review a new television commercial for Jell-O.

Eventually, I overcame my irritation and slowly I began to appreciate why we spent so much of our time at these meetings talking about marketing. Gradually it dawned on me that marketing was important—and that I had better learn more about it.

That was how my interest in marketing was aroused. Because I worked at General Foods, I had the opportunity to learn marketing from the experts. It was not by chance that General Foods had developed many of the world's leading consumer brands.

At General Foods, brand management was both an art and a science. I was fortunate to find myself in a position where I could absorb some highly valuable knowledge and then apply that knowledge to improve the performance of the IT organization.

I urge you to learn as much as you can about brand management and marketing. In addition to opening up new vistas for your career, the knowledge and skills you acquire will help you communicate the value of IT to your audience in terms that seem both natural and sincere.

The Medium is Still the Message

I am sure that you are already up to your ears in articles about social media, so I will touch only briefly on this topic. All I will say is this: Social media is not going away, so you might as well get used to using it.

Blogging and tweeting are easy ways to interact with your audiences on a regular basis. The types of interactions you engage in through social media do not have to be overly deep or personal. It is okay to be superficial. I have found that social media is a great way for reminding people that you are alive and well—and available in case they want to reach out to you in a more personal way.

What you blog and *what* you tweet is less important than the fact that you are using a highly potent form of information technology—the very technology that you as the CIO represent—to stay in touch with the rest of the world. Do not be afraid of looking foolish. Your audience will appreciate your effort, and they will reward you with greater loyalty and elevated respect.

"Corporate social media is an extension of the same trend we've been seeing on the Internet for a while—flattening hierarchies and connecting people across geographical distances," says Mitch Wagner, an executive editor at *Information Week*. "Social media, and especially applications like

Twitter, which is very easy to use, can make it easier for the CIO to find and connect people with common interests across large organizations."

Social media also can be used to improve the relationship between IT and the rest of the enterprise. "Communication between IT and the business units is a perennial issue within corporations," says Mitch. "Internal blogging can be a great tool for addressing that issue. You can blog internally about everything from security alerts to strategic IT initiatives. Basically it's a way of letting other people in the company know what's going on."

Here are four basic tips for successful blogging, courtesy of Mitch:

1. Blog regularly.

2. Blog in a conversational voice and avoid corporate-speak.

3. Invite and encourage interaction with your audience.

4. Be candid and admit mistakes when you make them.

Blog, tweets, and wikis are also great ways for uncovering shared interests and hidden talents across large groups of IT staffers working in multiple locations. From my perspective, anything that creates a sense of unity in a global IT department is a good thing.

I also see social media as a knowledge management tool that enables the CIO to tap into a vast reservoir of experience and insight that could easily be overlooked or undervalued.

Believe me, the people in your IT department are smart and they know things that you do not know. If social media can help you access some of their knowledge when you need it, I am all for it.

That being said, blogging is not easy. You should post several times a week, and for a busy CIO, that can be a burden. Even tweeting requires some effort, although not as much effort as writing a blog. Some CIOs designate an IT staffer to serve as their unofficial social media czar. I suspect that in the future, some CIOs might even hire someone on the basis of their ability to blog and tweet intelligently about IT. These are all ideas worth considering.

Some companies erect barriers to social media or impose stringent rules on using social networking platforms such as Facebook, mySpace, and Twitter. To be fair, companies in the health care and financial services industries, for example, are justifiably concerned about violating rules and regulations covering privacy, confidentiality, and the improper dissemination of information. I suggest working with your company's legal department to develop a clear set of guidelines that will enable you to blog and tweet without violating regulatory codes or running afoul of the law.

Generally, though, rules against using social media are both ineffective and silly. Worse, they send a clear signal to the rest of the world that your company is hopelessly behind the curve. Try not to let your company become one of *those* companies. This is a situation in which it makes good business sense to go with the flow.

As most of you are aware, Cisco uses social media to support and enable many of its global collaborative strategies. Cisco derives a double benefit from its innovative use of social media:

1. For Cisco, social media is a cost-effective way of sharing critical information and knowledge rapidly across a global enterprise.

2. The success of Cisco's social media initiatives promotes the products and services that Cisco sells to the rest of the world.

Here's the bottom line: Social media is definitely the new wave, so you might as well learn to surf in it.

Chapter 9

Building Relationships Across the Enterprise—And Beyond

Executive Summary

The CIO cannot accomplish everything alone. To make your IT and business strategies succeed, CIOs must build and manage relationships up, down, and sideways across the enterprise, and beyond the traditional boundaries. To earn the respect of peers and colleagues, the CIO must also demonstrate responsibility and accountability.

Earning Credibility

Much of the advice I have given in the previous chapters has focused on the goals a CIO must set, and the steps required to achieve them. But accomplishing those goals requires strength of personality. This type of strength flows from your ability to build and nourish personal relationships.

Darwin John, former CIO of the FBI, with previous high-level positions at the Mormon Church and the Scott Paper Company, says that the quality of a CIO's life is a function of the quality of his or her relationships. Developing these relationships takes time and energy. "It's something you can't force," he says.

I know that you have already heard this, but it is worth repeating: Your team is what gets you through good times and bad times. Your team must trust you and believe that you know what you are doing. If they do not trust you and believe in you, they will not be able to help you, no matter how talented and experienced they are.

Creating Relationships, One-on-One

I have a Facebook account. You can find me on LinkedIn. I even send tweets every now and then. But I believe strongly that the long-term, truly meaningful relationships you need to succeed in any business are created in an old-fashioned way: by one-on-one conversations, in person.

Motivating people is a big part of your job as CIO because your success depends on people far more than it depends on technology. Technology alone doesn't do anything; you need people who are trained and motivated to make the technology work for you and for the company.

At every company I worked for, I visited all our locations. *All of them.* I did not make these visits merely to investigate problems or evaluate opportunities that I had heard about. I made these visits—whether to Poland or New York City—to learn about the issues I *didn't* know about. Meeting with people face-to-face creates opportunities that justify the hassles of travel.

My in-person visits certainly had an impact on morale. Sometimes, people said, "This is the first time a CIO came to visit us." At one point in my career, I visited a call center in Arizona. After a tour, I spoke with the call center's team managers and then addressed the employees. If you are open and answer their questions honestly—you do not promise things that you cannot deliver or pretend that things are going great when they are not—these visits build respect. They also give you an opportunity to observe problems at the source.

Because you are not immersed in the problem, you may see things that the insiders do not.

Perhaps this sounds very political, as though my relationships are not genuine and are pursued only for what I will get out of it. But that's not the case. I have often become true friends with the people I meet in business because I communicate with sincerity. Yes, I have a reason to seek out some people, and I do my best to use my energy wisely, but the relationships are not fake. I made very good friends in Italy during the brief period that GM had a partnership with Fiat. When I went to Zaragoza, Spain, to speak with people at the GM plant there, I made instant friends. Some of the people I met on that visit now visit me at my home in Florida. I consider them great company—and not just because we once worked at the same company!

Intangible, But Also Valuable

I'm not the only person to feel this way about relationships. Eugene Nizker, managing partner of Evident Point Software in Vancouver, Canada, also recognizes the value of connecting with someone—in this case, a client—in a one-on-one relationship. The client was very upset, Nizker says, and believed he was being taken advantage of.

> *He hated everything that had any relation to our company, and had yelled at my CEO's assistant in coarse language. Many companies might cut off a client who behaved so unprofessionally, but this client was accountable for a significant chunk of our revenue.*

I was fresh to the company and thought he might have less reason to hate me, so I volunteered to deal with the client. My strategy was simple: The client is frustrated with what he considers our failure to deliver. Whether he is right or wrong, it is his perception hence his reality.

Our first conversations were not pretty. But I managed to stay calm. I didn't pick a fight no matter how hard he engaged me. I just answered his questions with straightforward and honest answers even when these answers were not pleasant. After half a dozen conversations (by e-mail and phone) we started to conduct normal, sane discussions, talking about matters of mutual concern. I provided the same information that he received before, but maybe in different form. He got the same level of transparency, but it was probably easier for him to trust a new face. We resolved the acute issues; I had solved our immediate problem. But it had long-term consequences that even I didn't predict.

A few weeks after the original conversations with the client, I met him face-to-face at a conference in London. He approached me with a hug.

The next month, we offered a few key clients (including this one) the opportunity to visit our offices and to audit our practices. A few days after the visit I received an e-mail that he sent to all our clients; he CCed me and the CEO. The client wrote that we were "worth every dollar he paid" to us. He became one of our greatest supporters and his testimonials have brought in significant new business.

I might do some things differently than Nizker—I would probably have flown to meet the client face-to-face, to start with—but his message is obvious. It is almost always worth the time to resolve situations rather than to walk away from them. Problems always become worse when you ignore them.

The one-on-one relationships help you run IT, but they can also benefit the business in unexpected ways.

Michael Hugos, principal at the Center for Systems Innovation, used to be the CIO of a national distribution cooperative. Networks Services Company sold a humble line of products: janitorial supplies and food service supplies (such as paper cups and plastic utensils). It's a business with plenty of competition, and the company wanted ways to differentiate itself so that it didn't have to compete on price alone.

Michael made an ally of the company's vice president of sales, going along on sales calls to listen to customer concerns and to determine if IT could help eliminate their problems.

I reached out to the CIO and the supply chain vice president at one of our biggest customers, a national chain of restaurants. Every holiday season they ran a special holiday promotion with a unique theme. We delivered products (such as paper cups and shopping bags) to their restaurants, printed with that year's holiday theme. Because the holiday theme changed every year, the customer had a great desire to use up all the special products. Any leftover products had to be written off. In prior years, they had $600,000 worth of excess inventory.

Our customer's supply chain vice president had embarked on a project to cut excess inventory by at least 50 percent. We did just that, by providing a suite of web-based systems to *watch the flow of inventory through the supply chain; it was used by the customer's operations managers, our offices, and at the holiday-item manufacturers who made these products. We also used our systems to help the customer forecast weekly demand during the season, to coordinate our delivery with store inventory, and provided information to the manufacturers to better schedule production in their factories. This suite of systems enabled much better collaboration and coordination than in previous years; in the first year alone we reduced excess inventory by more than $400,000.*

Michael's involvement in the supply chain solution enabled his company to win new multi-year supply contracts with the customer without having to reduce prices. The customer could measure the tangible benefits in the form of lower excess inventory costs and better supply chain operations. But the lesson is not his IT success story—it's the relationship success story.

This project was based upon the personal relationships I established. Without these relationships I would not have even known of the opportunity and I would not have had the trust or cooperation needed from other executives to deliver the system solutions that proved to be so effective.

Some of your most powerful relationships, certainly, begin inside your own company.

Role of the IT Board

I have already written at length about how much I depend on the IT Board to help me make good business and technology decisions. But first and foremost, the IT Board's intent is to streamline communication across the organization. The relationships you create here—both your personal connection with its members and the relationships the board members make amongst themselves—may be the most important.

A CIO's relationship with the IT Board is a two-way street. Don't make the mistake of seeing it as merely a "bully pulpit" from which you make pronouncements. It's an opportunity for you to share your expectations, but it's also the place where decisions are made and from which you learn the things you ought to know. The CIO runs the IT Board, but its members should feel that *they* are the company's IT function and that the IT Board's decisions control how IT operates.

Participating on the IT Board gets people to think outside their own silos and to cooperate with each other. Needless to say, this is not always easy. You may need to tell the IT Board, "Even if you are responsible for system development or for operations, when we discuss a strategy here I need everybody on the IT Board to contribute. When we make a decision, it's the IT Board's decision."

Before a decision is made—whether it's software selection or a new strategy to adopt virtualization across the data center—you should encourage a debate in which everyone's viewpoint is valid. IT board members should say whatever they think, and analyze and discuss the options. Everyone must also recognize that ultimately, the final decision will require some sort of compromise, but by then, most will understand and agree the decision was the best one for the time and situation.

Let's say you're choosing a software package for human resources. The responsible person does the legwork with the human resources group. She then presents the options to the IT Board and recommends one of the packages. Everybody on the board—the lawyer, the marketing gal, the operations guy—is questioned about the presentation. I go around the table, one-by-one, "How do you feel about this decision? What is your contribution here?"

At the end of the day, the decision is the CIO's responsibility. But sometimes I intentionally introduce a delay just to make sure that people work together. When people cannot seem to reach a conclusion, I've often said, "Why don't you three get together to work out the issues, and come up with a recommendation?" I could have made a decision without the extra work, but forcing them to work together enhances teamwork and lets them solve problems without relying on me to be tie-breaker all the time.

But after a decision is made, everybody on the team must be aligned with that decision. This is important. It doesn't matter what the decision was, whether the team member was for or against it. All the board members are responsible for the decision and it's now *our* decision, not someone else's.

There's another consequence to the IT Board making a decision: Everybody in that room becomes responsible for bringing the message down to their troops. The issue is not resolved when we have chosen a vendor or picked a new service-oriented architecture (SOA) strategy. Part of the IT Board's role is to discuss and resolve how to communicate the decision and move it forward. While you need to repeat your message yourself, you also must depend on others to reiterate the strategy and to take it for granted that *this* is the process the company will follow.

But communicating your message requires tailoring your messages for specific audiences. The details you will share with technical staffers, for example, will be different from the details you will share with front-line business managers.

If you work in a large, multinational company, cultural issues will affect the way you and your team communicate your strategy. People in New York City communicate differently than people in Atlanta. Western Europeans are different from Eastern Europeans, and South Asians are different from other Asians. Part of your job is taking all these differences into account and making sure that you are communicating effectively with all the various components of your audience. By necessity, that will require you to put more time and effort into developing and executing an effective communication strategy. But that is part of the modern CIO's job and there is no getting around it.

The more you understand the various cultural aspects of all the different kinds of people in IT, the better you can deliver your messages. IT people often *seem* independent of their native cultures because they tend to bond on the technical issues. But cultural differences exist, they are often powerful, and you need to be aware of them.

Sharing Power and Responsibility

When you are a CIO (or a CEO, for that matter), people expect you to know everything. That can be daunting, since we have to make decisions even in areas where we lack deep technical expertise.

This can make any CIO nervous, especially those who come from a technical background and who worry that they no longer understand the minutiae. If you started out as a programmer, you may feel guilty because you cannot write code as quickly as the kids fresh out of college. Get over it.

Instead of worrying about the things you don't know, build on the things you do know. If you were a crackerjack programmer back in the day, your background makes it easier for you to understand what motivates the programmers who work for you today.

CIOs have to work on multiple levels, each of which may require different skills. You need to think about the business and represent its technical needs. You also must understand both the big picture strategy and understand the people. But it doesn't mean that a CIO needs to know *everything*. The IT board can help you reduce a lot of the danger of making the wrong decision or making a decision based on only a few facts.

The CIO always brings the business perspective to the issue. I tell my team, "I act on your recommendations." I expect them to do the research, and then convince me—and the rest of the IT board—that their recommendation is the right one. The board, which includes other experts, makes the decision together. My role is to ask management questions of the technical staff: "If we make that decision, what are the consequences? How are we going to sell that? What is going to happen to the company? How would we transition to that?"

Learning the Business

The IT Board can help you make good decisions, but it also provides a venue for the CIO to interact with people who really understand the nuts and bolts of the business. That makes it especially valuable for CIOs who are new to a company and have to learn the business. Even if you do not have an IT Board, you should seek out people from whom you can learn and gather insight.

Darwin John, for example, moved from his CIO position in the Morman Church to the FBI; there's not a lot of commonality in their business processes! Sure, both organizations manage large databases and have plenty of IT needs in common, but there are vast differences between a church's human services and the business of law enforcement and intelligence gathering. He explains here.

The primary way I learned was to surround myself with people who knew the business all the way to the bottom. My leadership team had people who had come through the ranks as agents and had been in various roles. At any moment I could look to one of them and ask, "Okay, how does this work?"

Darwin wasn't shy about asking for help, and you should not be either.

I would approach people I wanted to earn credibility with, create relationships with, and build trust with. I'd say, "I'm the new kid on the block, help me understand this." Many felt good about tutoring me or mentoring me a bit. I drew on their generosity and learned; and at the same time in the process of that tutoring and mentoring, a relationship grew. The director (of the FBI) himself, was just very generous. He clearly wanted me to succeed.

Darwin's approach has been very successful. I go about learning in a slightly different way. When I arrive at a new organization, I delegate very little—at first.

For example, when I am new in an executive role, I tell my direct reports that nobody has the authorization to start any new project without my personal approval. I tell everyone that I want to know about every single project. This can create problems and occasional delays, because I have to sign off on every little change, but it actually helps me understand the company better than if I began delegating from day one. After I have learned what I need to know, then I can delegate and focus on my executive responsibilities.

Creating Relationships Upward

You cannot put your IT strategy in place unless the company board of directors buys into it.

Some CIOs adopt the attitude that the board of directors will decide what it wants, and they'll go along with their policy. In my experience, this never works. Instead, CIOs should take the initiative: Propose projects to the board and recommend the priority for each one. Occasionally, this brings a CIO into conflict with other members of the board, but that's part of the job. This should happen only occasionally, because ideally you have a relationship with the other people on the board.

This does not happen without effort. Determine who creates the opinions, the people who set the company direction, and work to understand their needs. If the financial director always controls the conversation about budgets, listen to her. Explain your plans, your strategies, your issues, and how you are dealing with them.

Review projects and plans with the influential people before board meetings. I met regularly with a smaller group (such as the CFO and the marketing vice president) to discuss project plans. It's an opportunity to get their input as well as sell them on your ideas. (If I couldn't get their support in a smaller meeting, I knew there was no point in presenting it to the board. This kept me from wasting time.)

Then, when the subject is discussed during the board meeting, those people are already briefed and can speak knowledgeably about your proposal. They are sold on how IT can help them solve their problems, and probably can explain the proposal as well as you can. If someone on the board offers a contrary opinion, your ally can answer the objections. This advantage cannot be overstated!

The relationships you create outside the board room—and outside the company—can also help you move your message forward. For example, I would participate in external CIO events, and bring back the ideas I learned to the company. I might emphasize or bring in line some of the things we were planning to do, and share how other companies were addressing similar challenges. Or I might participate in a CIO conference in which other CIOs were discussing how they were using social networks to help their businesses, and I would tell the board at my firm how that dovetailed with our own plans. That often helped to move along a project or to consolidate a strategy.

Managing and Delegating Across the Enterprise

As you build relationships across the company, you will discover what motivates the other departments and how IT can help them.

Chris Potts is a London-based corporate strategist. He previously held IT leadership positions in BUPA and AXA PPP Healthcare. Now he mentors CIOs in industry-leading companies worldwide. Over the course of his career, he has learned to appreciate the benefits and challenges of working with non-IT managers.

Potts once was introduced to a senior corporate strategist inside his organization. In their first meeting, Potts began the conversation by saying he wanted his help to "align the IT strategy with the business strategy." But the executive had no idea what he meant. Potts explains the situation.

The executive worked for an umbrella organization that owned a group of healthcare companies. There was no one single business strategy; rather, each business had its own individual strategy. However, the company also had an overall corporate strategy, plus some subject-area corporate strategies (such as finance, branding, and culture). No wonder he didn't understand what I wanted: There was no single strategy to align!

This didn't mean we couldn't work together. In fact, it was just the opposite. The strategist offered to explain each corporate strategy and to introduce me to the executive leading each one. When we in IT found that those corporate and business strategies were not aligned, we agreed not to take it on ourselves to fix those misalignments.

As the corporate strategist explained, the misalignments between individual strategies and the people leading them are normal, and create healthy tensions for the CEO to manage. If we in IT built our model of successful relationships on "alignment," then it was no surprise that we were struggling to be the creative force in the company.

That taught me to forget about "business–IT alignment." Instead, I found, it's more important to get involved in individual business and corporate strategies, and help to make them more successful because IT is involved. Remember you represent a corporate strategy too. And when you find that your strategy is misaligned with someone else's, remember that this is where the creative energy in strategies comes from.

Chris' experience highlights one of the lessons I've learned: It is important to ensure that the people in IT work as part of the business team. IT is only useful to the organization when it helps the business succeed, so your people have to be part of the business team's success.

This was always most obvious during portfolio prioritization. No matter how big the company is, budgets and resources are finite. Someone has to decide which IT projects are most important—and that usually comes out of a board of directors meeting.

I tell the IT teams that they have to meet with their business departments—marketing or manufacturing or whatever—to establish the priority of the projects for that area. Each team member, no matter how low on the organization chart, should ensure that his or her projects are well recognized within the business unit.

First, this forces the people in IT to have a relationship with the business. As you have learned by now, I think that is critical.

This also has an impact on setting project priority. If the business unit leaders are aware of the projects under consideration, they also know how important they are to their departments and are ready to defend the budget for them. By the time I make my priority recommendations to the board of directors, those leaders know the projects better than I do. They may disagree with the priorities I set, but they do so from knowledge, not based on hearsay.

Building Relationships with Vendors

For many CIOs, relationships with vendors are often adversarial. In the CIO's eyes, the vendor wants something from the company (usually more money) and the CIO wants to protect the company from harm. In reality, however, vendors can help you move your strategy forward.

When you rely on an individual in your organization—say, the application development manager—you talk with her frequently. Understanding only blooms in the presence of communication, and the more one-on-one the relationship, the more effective we can all be.

The same general rule applies to vendors. When you rely on them, you have to talk with them frequently, too. Every month, I met with my top suppliers to explain my IT plan and the company's strategies. I'd tell them outright what I wanted to accomplish, and I would listen to their answers about how they might help me do so.

Your vendors can also help you communicate your message. Because the vendors interact with other people in your company, they can repeat your strategy. For example, if the CEO of one of my major vendors wanted to meet with my company's CEO—a plum opportunity for the vendor's CEO—I was perfectly willing to help arrange a meeting. I never had an issue with this. But I told my vendor contact, "You have to tell my story to them." I expect a vendor who meets with my CEO to support my strategy and reinforce my message.

For example, if I had formed an IT strategy to move my IT organization toward cloud computing, I would expect the vendor CEO to tell my boss that cloud computing is the right choice. Naturally, the vendor CEO will also tell my boss that his company is uniquely positioned to provide a relevant solution, but that is to be expected.

In Chapter 4, I gave you another demonstration of how to build a vendor relationship: meeting with a vendor after a problem is resolved. As you'll remember from that chapter, once the emergency is over, I met with all the vendors involved to find out what had happened, what lessons we learned, and what actions to take as a result.

Most companies have these discussions behind closed doors; I involved the vendors in these discussions because I knew it would be helpful to have them in the room.

I should warn you that this is not successful with every vendor. They may complain that this sort of interaction is not covered by their contract (though ideally, it is). If they complain, I reply, "I don't care if we have a contract or not; you guys are here to make sure that this stuff works all the time, everywhere, in the company. You are an extended part of my IT department."

I have also told them, "Your mission is to make us look good. If this stuff is not working or the project is late, we are not looking good." They get the message.

Developing vendor relationships is a crucial part of your role as CIO. *You* are responsible for making *them* responsible for serving your organization and for making them part of your continuous improvement process.

Getting and Staying On Message

Among the first TV programs I watched after I arrived in the United States was a presidential debate in which Ronald Reagan participated. People asked him all kinds of hairy questions with no way out. I watched Mr. Reagan turn those debate questions into answers that helped him convey his message. Whether you agree with his policies is beside the point; I want to emphasize how well he transformed an "attack" question into something he could use. President Obama does the same thing. Getting "on message" and staying there is very much part of being a leader.

You can't just set a strategy; you need other people to support it and to deliver on it. A CIO should take every opportunity to educate employees, vendors, and the company at large. When you speak with the board of directors or interview the newest developer on your team, they need to believe your assertions and they must be very clear about your intentions.

That's not just a matter of people nodding along when you stand at a conference podium and clapping politely at the end of your speech. Earlier, I wrote about the difficult necessities of negotiating with vendors in order to keep costs manageable. At some point you may need to tell people, "We are negotiating with a vendor who is charging us absurd prices. I know that you currently use the vendor's products, and I know that the vendor will try to approach you directly. I need your support, and I expect your support."

As the CIO, you should be utterly certain that everyone—from department managers to end users—will adhere to the business strategy you set. If you communicate your strategy carefully and clearly, and if you also demonstrate the logic and the reasoning behind it, people will be more likely to follow your lead.

Good leaders influence and motivate people to achieve their goals. I believe that when people feel successful, they also feel grateful to the person who enabled their success. Gratitude, I believe, inspires loyalty and loyalty is like money in the bank. Sooner or later you will need to draw on it to accomplish *your* goals.

Make Sure That Everyone Knows That You Are Responsible and Accountable

Part of the way in which executives build relationships is by demonstrating their value to other executives.

If you want to sit at the executive table, you need to earn respect from the other C-level executives in the enterprise. The best way to earn their respect is by consistently demonstrating that you are responsible and accountable for everything related to IT.

The most straightforward way of demonstrating this is by making sure that IT always meets or exceeds expectations. IT must deliver on the promises that you make, or you will lose the respect of the executive team. Once this respect is lost, it is awfully difficult to regain. And since respect is the foundation of all relationships, I urge you strongly to guard and protect it zealously. If you miss deadlines and exceed budgets, you will squander the respect you need to accomplish your objectives as CIO.

Chapter 10

Act Like a CEO

Executive Summary

IT is a business within a business. The CIO is the CEO of this business. Since you already are, for all intents and purposes, a chief executive, you might as well act like one. When you act like a CEO, you elevate the role of IT. Your job also becomes more interesting and more rewarding. Who knows? Maybe you will become your company's next CEO.

Climbing the Ziggurat

For many years I have felt fortunate to be a member of the global information technology community. From my humble beginnings as an accounting student in São Paulo to my post as CIO of General Motors Europe, my life has been an exciting adventure. My career has had its ups and downs, to be sure. But the successes I have achieved relied less on my ability to master complex technologies and more on my willingness to learn the art of executive leadership.

In short, my success was built upon my executive leadership skills. My ability to improve and refine those executive skills over time is what really kept me in the game.

I never became a CEO. My destiny took me in another direction, and I have no regrets. Sometimes promotion is a matter of luck and timing. In retrospect, perhaps it was just as well that I did not become the CEO of any of the companies I worked for.

When I began writing this book, one of my goals was helping CIOs become better executives. I assumed, as I still do, that becoming a better executive would lead a CIO to higher levels of success in his or her career.

I also wanted to help CIOs make their jobs more interesting, more rewarding, more fun and, quite frankly, more important. I wanted to help CIOs prepare themselves for promotion to what I see as the next logical step for them, the role of CEO.

I know of only a handful of CIOs who have become CEOs. But I do not believe there is a "glass ceiling" preventing CIOs from being promoted to positions of greater authority and responsibility; I see no reason why more CIOs cannot become CEOs. Indeed, I would argue that because CIOs must be familiar with all areas of the company, they are already positioned to become great CEOs.

In this chapter, I will argue that the CIO has as much right to seek the coveted corner office as any other C-level executive. But I will also discuss some of the steps the CIO must take, and some of the challenges the CIO must overcome to ascend to the next level.

The Business Within the Business

From my perspective as a former global CIO, I tend to see IT as a business within a larger business. I am certainly not the first person to make this observation, but it is worth repeating. The previous chapters all contain examples and anecdotes implicitly supporting the idea that IT, unlike other functional areas of the enterprise, operates optimally when it is managed like a free-standing business, and operates sub-optimally when it is managed like a service center.

I honestly cannot remember when I realized that the ideal CIO is in fact the CEO of a business called IT. But somewhere along the line this idea occurred to me, and I have tried to act like the CEO of a business ever since.

To a surprising degree, many of the IT functions discussed in the previous chapters mirror the functions of the enterprise. (See Exhibit 10.1.)

CIOs who did make it to the corner office were successful because they understood that IT *is* a business, and they learned how to act like the CEO. I have a strong hunch that any CIO who runs IT like a business will have a better shot at becoming CEO than a CIO who runs IT like a service center.

Exhibit 10.1   IT Functions Reflect Enterprise Business Functions

Enterprise Functions	IT Functions
Product Development	Application and Services Development
Engineering	Architecture
Sales and Marketing	Promoting and Marketing IT
Operations	IT Production

Why You Need to Behave Like a CEO

Even if you have no desire or ambition to be promoted from CIO to CEO, you still have to act like a CEO.

I firmly believe that in today's complex business environment, acting like a CEO cannot be considered optional behavior. Acting like a CEO is a cultural imperative for every C-level officer, and it is especially important for the CIO.

CEOs tend to be people who understand intuitively how to win the trust and confidence of other people. I would argue that in a modern organization, one of the CEO's primary functions is inspiring trust and confidence.

In fact, the ability to inspire trust and confidence is precisely what the board of directors looks for when hiring a new CEO, especially during difficult times such as these.

Because the board knows that the CEO will be able to lead the organization ONLY after gaining the trust and confidence of all the people inside and outside of the company whose good faith and cooperation are required to achieve the company's strategic business goals.

Trust and confidence are not buzzwords—they are the glue that keeps the organization from flying apart under tremendous pressure. No senior executive can function effectively for very long without cultivating the ability to inspire trust and confidence.

That is why is it critical for the CIO to behave like a CEO. You must be capable of inspiring trust and confidence.

Now here is the rub: You will start off at a disadvantage. There is no getting around this disadvantage, so we must discuss it openly.

People who do *not* understand technology tend to feel uncomfortable around people who *do* understand technology. And people who have been around long enough to remember the bad old days when the IT department was a mysterious organization operating in a sealed room in the basement are not likely to become your natural allies.

Yes, it is true that most of the young people today have an intuitive grasp of technology; they are plugged in, quite literally, to all of their digital devices. So they will be on your side.

But at this moment, Generation Y is not your primary challenge. Many of the people whose support you will need will be Baby Boomers and Gen Xers—people who might not be entirely comfortable with the idea of a CIO acting like a CEO.

So the CIO starts off with a disadvantage. Some people are inclined to mistrust the CIO and some people are inclined to be fearful of IT. As a result, the CIO needs to go *above and beyond* to overcome these prejudices.

Take a Step Back

One of your critical responsibilities as CIO is helping the CEO to grow the business. But focusing solely on growth can lead to bad decisions. You need to step back, take a deep breath and look carefully at the business you are trying to grow. Ask yourself if you really understand all the various parts of the business that are crucial to its growth.

Do you understand the fundamentals of the business? Do you understand the needs and demands of its customers? How much do you know about its channel partners?

Do you understand the history and dynamics of the industry your business competes in? Do you understand the characteristics of the various markets your business competes in?

Do you think about all the ways in which new technologies can help the business grow? Are you looking for new markets and new opportunities that will enable the business to grow?

After you have taken that important step back and really looked hard at the business, you will be in a better position to identify and articulate innovative strategies that can help the business. You will know enough about the business and its markets to pitch ideas and proposals to the company board with confidence and assurance.

Remember, when you pitch an idea and it's accepted, the chances are good that you will be chosen to implement it.

That means more responsibility, more authority, more visibility and more opportunity for you.

My point is this: Sometimes taking a step back can put you one step closer to becoming CEO.

Style *Is* Important

In 2005, Korn/Ferry International released an executive report entitled, "CIO to CEO." The report's authors were Mark Polansky and Simon Wiggins. They based their text on data gathered by Korn/Ferry on more than a half-million top executives (nearly 1,500 of whom were senior-level IT leaders). The data was analyzed and mined to develop "success profiles" for the positions of CIO, CEO, and chief operating officer (COO).

I am bringing this report to your attention because it deals specifically with key behavioral differences between CIOs, COOs, and CEOs. I believe that it is important to be aware of these differences. Once you are aware of them, you can choose to alter or modify your behavior and improve your chances of success.

For example, while the leadership styles of CIOs, COOs, and CEOs seem similar on the surface, the underlying thought processes of the three types of executives are different enough to warrant your consideration.

"...CIOs are by custom, training, and experience much more analytical...than their CEO/COO colleagues,"

Polansky and Wiggins. The CIO "requires complex and creative problem-solving skills that are long-term in orientation..."

In other words, the typical CIO does not have the luxury of making snap judgments—even when those judgments might prove beneficial.

To avoid making costly mistakes, the CIO is often forced to seek haven in a relatively safe middle ground between stated internal objectives and unpredictable external realities.

It is easy to see how a CIO can become accustomed to acting slowly, deliberatively, and scrupulously. Sometimes it seems as though the words "due diligence" have been branded indelibly into the CIO's subconscious.

The report notes that for CEOs and COOs, the "call to action" comes so quickly that often there is no time for analysis or introspection. Responses must be immediate and forceful—even if they are not always effective or productive.

CIOs, however, "...face incredible and endless changes in IT systems and developments. In essence, they spend their careers responding to tactical challenges where there is typically less room to maneuver, fewer practical options and hence, less control."

Polansky and Wiggins are not pessimistic, however, about the potential for CIOs to move beyond their traditional roles and ascend into higher management posts. They point out that CIOs, COOs, and CEOs tend to "share most of the be-havioral qualities that are generally held as critical for success in business" and that "technology executives diverge from the pack in small but significant respects."

"The most obvious differences between CIOs and other top executives," write Polansky and Wiggins, "are the speed at which they arrive at decisions when placed under pressure" and "the manner in which they communicate their decisions to the people around them."

I found this piece of advice from Polansky and Wiggins especially useful:

> *CIOs aspiring to become COOs or CEOs must evaluate their capacity for behavioral change. If the CIO is confident that such change can be made, then he or she should focus on developing a leadership style that more closely matches the action-oriented style of the most senior executives and eschews some of the more analytic qualities that are commonly as-sociated with successful technology executives. The CIO must adopt the attitudes and styles of strategic leadership, and be willing to leave the tactical details to others.*

Now that we have looked in the mirror, what can we do? As mentioned earlier, this kind of self-awareness is useful even if you are not grooming yourself to become the next CEO. The point is that in order to function successfully as a CIO, you must adopt the characteristics of a CEO. In good times and bad, I am convinced that doing anything less is an invitation to failure.

Do Not Forget Altruism

Sometimes I think there was a good angel sitting on my shoulder during this book project. For instance, when I asked my friend Mike Barlow to find some good articles about the role of the CEO, he contacted a friend who connected him to Rita Gunther McGrath.

Many of you already know Rita. She is the co-author of three excellent books published by Harvard Business School Press, *The Entrepreneurial Mindset* (2000), *MarketBusters: 40 Strategic Moves that Drive Exceptional Business Growth* (2005) and *Discovery Driven Growth* (2009). She has a doctorate from the University of Pennsylvania's Wharton School and she teaches at Columbia Business School in New York.

Rita's deep understanding of strategy and operations—two disciplines that are rapidly merging into one unified *gestalt*—makes her a wonderful source of knowledge for this discussion.

"The CEO's role is focusing the energy and attention of the organization. The CEO determines what's really important and who gets the resources," Rita says.

A CIO who wants to act like a CEO must be willing to make decisions and establish priorities. Both of these chores are demanding, and both are fraught with risks. In many situations, there is no single right answer and no clearly defined path that can be followed. Taking risks is part of the job, however, and it cannot be avoided.

But here is an important point: People must perceive that you are taking these risks to help the business. In other words, they must believe that you are taking risks to improve their chances for success. On some level, you must allow them to sense your altruism.

I know this probably sounds "touchy feely," but I assure you that is not my intention. Altruism is the foundation of collaboration, and you will not be able to inspire the kind of teamwork required to operate a modern organization without first establishing your bona fides as a caring human being.

You must be prepared to demonstrate that you are willing to take risks for the organization and that you care about the people within the organization. This might seem like an impossible task, but it is not. Difficult, yes. Impossible, no.

Outside versus Inside

Rita also recommended "What Only the CEO Can Do," an article by A.G. Lafley that appeared recently in the *Harvard Business Review*. Lafley is the former CEO of Procter & Gamble, and I believe that he has emerged as one of the true geniuses of modern management.

I urge you to read his article, which examines specific tasks that can be accomplished only by the CEO and no one else. Lafley's article led me to "The American CEO," an earlier article by Peter Drucker that was published in *The Wall Street Journal* in 2005.

In his article, Drucker argues that in addition to deciding priorities, the CEO must serve as the link between the "Inside" of the organization and the "Outside" of the organization. From Drucker's perspective, the "Outside" includes markets, customers, the media, and society at large.

The CEO's primary task, according to Drucker, is defining "the meaningful Outside . . . but the definition is anything but easy, let alone obvious."

Drucker believed that every organization would have its own unique definition of "meaningful Outside" and that only the CEO could decide precisely what that definition was.

The CEO's next critical task, Drucker wrote, "is to think through what information regarding the Outside is meaningful and needed for the organization, and then work on getting it into usable form."

After, and only after, the CEO has accomplished these tasks can the next critical questions be raised: What is our business and what results are meaningful for us?

If we take Drucker's vision and apply it to our discussion about the CIO, the "inside" becomes the IT organization and the "outside" is the rest of the enterprise. The CIO, therefore, is the link between IT and the enterprise.

The CIO's job is defining the enterprise and then figuring out how to gather the information that will enable IT to achieve results in that "meaningful Outside."

As you can see, this involves a lot more work than choosing an accounts receivable solution or deciding whether to outsource a call center. But after four decades in IT, I am convinced that the CIO's role is much more than administering systems.

As Rita says, some CIOs do not seem overly interested in the business. They seem content to focus on the problems and challenges within IT. I understand their reluctance to grapple with the issues outside of IT. But I also think that they are missing the big picture.

If IT is your primary focus, then you are looking only at the "Inside," as Drucker might say. "Inside, there are only costs. Results are only on the Outside," wrote Drucker. "Indeed the modern organization . . . was expressly created to have results on the Outside, that is, to make a difference in its society or its economy."

If you want to make a difference, you must look outside of IT. You must become the interface between IT and the enterprise. Only then can you help the enterprise achieve its goals.

Find the Middle Ground

As much as I admire Peter Drucker, I am going to close the book with some advice from my friend Marco Stefanini. Marco believes in seeking the middle ground and avoiding extremes. Back in Chapter 5, he suggested an approach to contracting that balances global and regional needs. I think this is a very intelligent approach that deserves more consideration than it is usually given.

Marco suggests taking a similar approach when you are confronted by the need to make decisions about newer technologies. For example, instead of diving head-first into cloud computing, first determine which parts of the business are likely to benefit and which are not.

Cloud computing is probably a great choice for relatively low-risk applications such as sales contact management, marketing and e-mail. But you probably would not want to migrate your ERP or manufacturing systems into the cloud any time soon.

Remember also that any newer technologies you embrace will have to work alongside older technologies, so plan for a period of transition. As you are well aware, nothing in IT happens overnight. The transition to cloud computing may be inevitable, but it will take years to accomplish. You do not have to be the leader in every area of IT; sometimes it is better to stay with the pack and let others do the "testing."

In fact, why not let your suppliers help you explore new technologies? From the supplier's perspective, newer technologies might not generate as much profit as their existing solutions, but they should be willing to help you test the waters by offering low-risk solutions that incorporate some features or aspects of newer technologies.

This kind of moderate approach is also good for your suppliers, because it gives them a good reason to experiment and innovate. In the process, they might come up with the next killer app.

At the very least, you will have pushed the envelope without actually tearing it. And that brings me neatly to my final point: As the CIO, you have a responsibility to be cool and courageous, no matter how dire the circumstances. But you also have a responsibility to make choices that will stand the tests of time. So my advice is to be brave, but also be prudent. The two are not incompatible, and I have every confidence that if you look hard enough, you will find the middle ground that enables you to be both.

AFTERWORD

Jim Giustini
Director, Resources Global Professionals

"We just experienced a complete outage at our datacenter which lasted over three hours. I have ten days to figure out what went wrong and determine how we can prevent this from happening again. Is this something you can help us with?"

The unexpected call I received from José Eiras that Saturday afternoon led to one of the most interesting consulting projects of my career and, more importantly, the opportunity to develop a relationship with one of the most intriguing executives I've ever met.

If I had to pinpoint what is unique about José, I would have to say it is his global perspective. Not global just in the geographical or multicultural sense of the word (although he is a Harvard-educated Brazilian who speaks five languages, and has lived and worked around the world). I mean a perspective that is *comprehensive* or *complete*.

For me, one of the key messages of this book is the importance of expanding one's viewpoint. In the case of our collaboration in the root cause analysis of the datacenter outage mentioned above, for instance, the global or holistic perspective required was to think beyond technology infrastructure to also examine related process and organizational factors.

This theme is repeated throughout the book: The importance of looking outside of IT, getting comfortable with numbers, being a collaborator with business rather than acting as an order taker. It is through an expanded perspective that CIOs become strategists, leaders, motivators, marketers, and relationship managers. As José suggests, they begin to think of IT as a business and themselves as CEOs.

You hear all the time about CEOs and CFOs having a certain unique management style. I've come to believe that it is actually CIOs who vary the most in terms of their backgrounds, specific strengths, and leadership styles.

In my personal experience, people often seem to think that CIOs are essentially interchangeable. This view could prove to be dangerous. At CIO transition points, in particular, it would serve CEOs and board members well to invest a little more time matching the company's current set of *business* priorities (and not just technology goals) to the corresponding attributes most necessary and desirable in their next CIO. One potentially powerful use of José's insights is for the development of criteria to effectively screen, evaluate, and select future CIOs. Aspiring CIOs can also leverage the practical advice in this book to map out a learning path for their careers.

Can you teach old CIO dogs new tricks? I imagine most CIOs are already employing some, if not many, of the concepts outlined in the preceding pages. But the desire to significantly and proactively enhance one's effectiveness or broaden one's perspective surely requires a certain degree of passion and curiosity.

It is one thing for a CIO to have a solid grasp of the company's IT cost structure, for example. That's expected and required. However, it is probably a much smaller subset of CIOs who have an excellent understanding of the operating costs of the entire organization and frequently look to identify new ways the IT organization can help improve *operational* efficiency or dramatically impact customer satisfaction without being prodded to do so.

I guess passion and curiosity aren't things we learn. Maybe the best we can do is to make a little room for them in our lives, and cultivate them when they naturally appear. A trip to Brazil probably wouldn't hurt either.

ENDNOTES

General Note

Most of this book is based on my own experiences as a corporate executive. My career spanned four decades and carried me to many exotic locales all over the world. It also put me in contact with hundreds of highly intelligent people, all of whom influenced me in one way or another. In retrospect, it is not surprising that I learned a lot from my bosses, colleagues, and peers. More importantly, I learned a lot—and owe a lot—to the people who worked for me. Much of the knowledge I acquired over the course of my career has become so deeply embedded in my personality that I am no longer even aware of it on a conscious level. Writing this book was a little bit like digging with a shovel through an old mine. I knew there were precious gems down there, but I was not sure exactly where they were buried. Fortunately I was able to find many of them with the help of my editorial director, Mike Barlow. Each discovery, it seemed, guided us to a new cache of thoughts and memories, and inspired the writing of yet another chapter.

Introduction

A good portion of the Introduction appeared initially in a column that I had written for CIO.com in early 2009. The column itself was based on a presentation that I had made before a group of CIOs the previous year. The presentation had been an attempt to formulate a series of practical steps that CIOs could follow to survive the global economic meltdown. Later I realized that many of the steps that I had outlined in the presentation would be useful in any type of economic circumstances.

Chapter 1: Build a Great Team

Most of the content in this chapter was derived from personal recollections from various stages in my career, and from presentations that I had developed to build high-level IT teams. For example, I had created the list of IT competencies for an earlier presentation. Exhibit 1.1 showing the composition of a typical IT Board is based on charts that I used to build IT teams at GM Latin America, Europe, and also at DHL. The quotes from my former GM colleagues, Robin Watson and Alejandro Martinez, and from Harvey Koeppel, formerly CIO of Citigroup's Global Consumer Group, were gleaned from separate telephone interviews conducted in early 2009. The quotes from Coach K are used with his permission.

Chapter 2: Proactively Establish Goals for IT

This chapter is based almost entirely on my recollections of events that occurred during my tenure at GM, Philip Morris, and earlier while I was beginning my career at Kibon in Brazil.

Chapter 3: Design the IT Strategy

This chapter is based largely on ideas that had been percolating in my mind from the earliest days of my first management job. Gradually over time these ideas evolved into my own set of "best practices" for strategy development and executive leadership. The quotes and anecdotes from Jim Onalfo, my mentor at General Foods, were gathered during the course of several in-depth interviews conducted in June 2009. The strategy exhibits represent my own original efforts to develop a practical framework for IT strategy formulation.

Chapter 4: Hold All of Your Vendors Accountable

Most of the content for this chapter is based on recollections of my experiences at GM and DHL. The quotes and anecdotes from Beth Kirkpatrick, a former GM colleague, were gathered from an in-depth telephone interview conducted in April 2009.

Chapter 5: Before Negotiating, Do Your Homework

A good chunk of this chapter was derived from an in-depth telephone interview in June 2009 with Bob Turner, the CEO of Smart Software Deals, LLC. Bob also appears briefly in *Partnering with the CIO* by Michael Minelli and Mike Barlow (John Wiley & Sons, 2007). The suggestions from Marco Stefanini were gleaned from a telephone interview conducted in October 2009.

Chapter 6: Manage Contracts, Don't Just Sign Them

This chapter is based largely on my recollections of events that occurred while I was the CIO of General Motors Latin

America. The chapter also contains excellent advice from my friend, Claude Marais of TPI, Inc., a global sourcing advisory firm. Claude's quotes and commentary were gathered from an in-depth telephone interview conducted in June 2009. Jim Onalfo related the "eyeball-to-eyeball" anecdote (about the meeting between his boss at General Foods and the IBM executive responsible for the global IT integration effort) during an in-person interview in June 2009.

Chapter 7: Work With the Business

The first half of this chapter is based largely on an in-depth telephone interview with Manjit Singh of Chiquita Brands conducted in August 2009. The interview with Manjit really got me thinking about all the useful lessons that CIOs can learn from consumer packaged goods companies. The anecdotes and stories from Steve Marenakos of Prudential were gathered from a telephone interview conducted in June 2009. The commentary and insight from Ashlee Aldridge of West Marine were gleaned from a July 2009 telephone interview.

Chapter 8: Manage and Market the IT Brand

This chapter is based largely on my recollection of efforts and initiatives that I had began at GM, Philip Morris, and DHL. It also relies on material gathered from an in-depth telephone interview conducted in July 2009 with my former GM colleague Tony Scott. Tony, as many of you know, is now the CIO of Microsoft. This chapter also benefits greatly from information gathered from an in-depth telephone interview conducted in July 2009 with Mansour Zadeh of Smithfield Foods. The general advice on blogging and other forms of social media emerged from my conversations with Mike Barlow in August 2009 and from a telephone interview with journalist Mitch Wagner conducted in September 2009.

Chapter 9: Build Relationships Across the Enterprise—and Beyond

In addition to my own thoughts and recollections, the penultimate chapter is based largely on material collected from telephone interviews with Darwin John, former CIO of the FBI; Eugene Nizker of Evident Point Software; Michael Hugos of the Center for Systems Innovation; and Chris Potts, a corporate strategist based in London. Esther Schindler, the noted writer and blogger, also provided valuable insight and advice.

Chapter 10: Act Like a CEO

The main thrust of this chapter emerges from my own reflections and ruminations. Looking back on my career, I realized that a good deal of my success depended more on my executive skills and less on my technology skills. I think this is an important point and I wanted to share it with others who seek a similar path. Mike Barlow uncovered the useful Korn/Ferry report, "CIO to CEO," and the quotes from it are used with permission. The chapter also benefits from a brief telephone interview conducted with Rita Gunther McGrath in June 2009. Additionally, the chapter cites two excellent articles: "What Only the CEO Can Do," an article by A.G. Lafley that appeared in the *Harvard Business Review* in 2009; and "The American CEO," an article by Peter Drucker that was published in *The Wall Street Journal* in 2005. The useful advice from Marco Stefanini was culled from a telephone interview conducted in October 2009.

ABOUT THE AUTHOR

José Carlos Eiras is a global CIO with extensive experience in the food, tobacco, automobile, transportation, and distribution industries, and he has worked for businesses on every continent across the globe. As an accomplished technology leader and an agent of change, Eiras is highly regarded for his ability to transform IT technology for Fortune 10 global companies, creating long-term competitive advantages in rapidly changing markets.

He was recently Chief Information Officer of DHL Express-US, a division of Deutsche Post World Net (DPWN), the world's leading logistics and transportation company. He was recruited to DHL Express to drive IT initiatives to turn around and build the package delivery business in the United States, competing with Federal Express and UPS.

Previously, Eiras had served as CIO Latin America, Africa, and Middle East (LAAM) for General Motors (GM). One of his tasks was assuming IT responsibilities previously handled by EDS, which GM had divested in 1996. His experience and leadership is credited for building a strong internal IT discipline, replacing EDS and then managing EDS as a supplier, which was a major benefit for GM LAAM. In parallel, Eiras developed strategies and executed plans that replaced most of GM LAAM's old systems infrastructure with a SAP-based solution.

Following his success in LAAM, Eiras was appointed CIO General Motors Europe where he was responsible for bringing together a disparate and culturally diverse IT group located in several countries. He developed long-term systems strategies by functional area and integrated each with business strategies, propelling General Motors Europe systems and IT infrastructure ahead of its automotive competitors. This success was achieved through the implementation of engineering systems and tools, sales, service and marketing systems, and web portals, along with, manufacturing, quality supply chain, finance, and human resources systems. Eiras also deployed packages such as SAP, PeopleSoft, and Siebel. At the same time he reduced IT structural costs by more than 30 percent in four years and increased investment in IT infrastructure, security, and new applications.

After five years in Europe, Eiras was appointed Global Services Information Officer with responsibilities for General Motors' worldwide IT infrastructure and services and implemented global services contracts, with several tier-one suppliers, covering all aspects of the IT infrastructure.

Prior to General Motors, he was appointed Latin America Systems Director for Philip Morris. Earlier in his career, Eiras held positions of increasing responsibility at Kraft Foods in Brazil, the United States, and Spain. He attributes his success to strong leadership abilities in business and IT.

Eiras earned an equivalent MBA degree from Harvard Business School and earlier a BA from Escola Superior, a branch of the Catholic University in São Paulo, Brazil. In his free time Eiras enjoys soccer, golf, and travel with his family.

For more information, updated content and additional materials, please visit www.thepracticalcio.com and www.josecarloseiras.com.

INDEX